Carol Vance Wary

Wild Game Cookery

THE HUNTER'S HOME COMPANION

D1509139

THE COUNTRYMAN PRESS ▼ WOODSTOCK, VERMONT

To my children who have given my life purpose, to my family who have been my strength, and to all my outdoor writer friends without whom I would not be writing a third book. A special thanks also, to the writers and friends who have generously contributed their recipes and time to this expanded volume.

AUTHOR'S ACKNOWLEDGMENTS

I am grateful to Mr. Joe Cahn and The New Orleans School of Cooking for allowing his recipes to be adapted for use with wild game and included here. Thanks are also due to Freida Products of California for allowing the use of the marketing term "Sunchokes" in reference to the Jerusalem artichoke. Dover Publications, Inc. kindly granted permission to reproduce a number of illustrations from *Food and Drink: A Pictorial Archive from Nineteenth-Century Sources* (second revised edition, 1980).

Library of Congress Cataloging-in-Publication Data
Wary, Carol Vance.
  Wild game cookery : the hunter's home companion / Carol Vance Wary.—[Rev., expanded ed.]
    p.   cm.
    ISBN 0-88150-111-5 (pbk.)
    1. Cookery (Game)   I. Title.
TX751.W37   1988
641.6'91—dc19   88-2728
                                                                                        CIP

Cover and text design by Leslie Fry
Photocomposition by N.K. Graphics
Printed in the United States of America

A PERSONAL NOTE
TO THE READER

For over twenty years my family and I have lived on two secluded acres in the heart of the lush Lehigh Valley near Allentown, Pennsylvania. The setting has enhanced my exposure to wildlife, for our woods and fields abound with wild game. The pastoral surroundings have also been the source of great comfort these many years after the emotionally demanding job of teaching third grade.

I must admit that my initial efforts at preparing wild game were not always as successful as I would have liked them to be, but as exposure and experience with food grew, so did my expertise.

It seems that nature has prevented me from ever following a recipe as written. I always think, well, this could stand some dill, or, I bet cheese would enhance this. Trial, error, experimentation, and lots of determination have, over the years, produced recipes that make wild game meals not just good, but outstanding.

I knew my wild game dishes had truly arrived when my daughter and son-in-law wanted Kahlua Quail, Venison Fingers, and Elegant Pheasant at their wedding reception. It was a compliment I will always cherish.

This book is a complete guide to the preparation of game. It contains kitchen-tested recipes that include venison, bear, large game animals, small game, fowl, and wild vegetables. I have also included some of my family favorites in the "Down

Home" section. There are ideas for appetizers, main dishes, and family suppers, as well as haute cuisine. With this book, Chinese, German, and Italian foods can be prepared from the hunter's bounty using many secrets learned in my mother's kitchen and my father's butcher shop.

As you read my cookbook, keep in mind that all these recipes were adapted from those used cooking with domestic meats, so do try them with beef and chicken and pork. I'd like you to use this book until the pages are dog-eared and some of them even stick together, a sure sign that marks a favorite.

Wild game needs a little extra attention to be tender and tasty to the average person. Recent studies show that all game is much healthier than domestic varieties because of its low fat content. Game prepared well, pleasing to the palate, and healthful, too, should make enthusiastic diners of us all.

Large Game

VENISON

Venison is the meat of any of the antlered members of the deer family, that is moose, elk, antelope, caribou, mule deer and white-tailed deer. The whitetail ranges throughout most of the United States from the southern border of Canada southward through Mexico, Central America, and into South America as far as Peru and Bolivia. Because of this broad geographical distribution, a number of variations in size, color, and habits have developed, and a dozen or more species and subspecies of white-tailed deer are recognized scientifically.

The size of a deer depends to a great extent on environment and food. The largest white-tailed deer inhabit the northeastern woodlands of the United States and Canada. Some of the biggest whitetails on record have been taken in the Adirondack Mountains of New York State and throughout Northern New England. Huge bucks, weighing as much as 400 pounds, have been recorded, with the average weight of a mature male being around 250 to 300 pounds. The smallest deer in North America are found in Mexico, where maximum weight of a mature buck is only 40 pounds. In the Florida Keys a mature male Key deer rarely exceeds 80 pounds.

The general form of the antlers, the color and size of the tail, and the size of a scent gland on each hind leg are characteristics that help to distinguish the white-tailed deer from other members of its subgenus.

American Indians and Eskimos hunted deer long before the white man settled in the western hemisphere. They used its flesh for food and its bones and antlers for fashioning crude tools and weapons. Primitive people in Europe and Asia used their deer species in similar ways. The Laplanders of northern Europe still are dependent on their reindeer for milk, meat, clothing, housing, and transportation. Laplanders have a low incidence of heart disease and cholesterol problems.

Deer have been of great use to man throughout civilization and still represent an important part of our economy. State wildlife bureaus receive a substantial income from the fees charged for hunting licenses, enabling them to support the departments in charge of game management. The hunting "industry," generally, is a large employer when one considers all its aspects. The number of men and women necessary to produce the vast amount of equipment required by the hunters of our country is staggering. The total expenditures on licenses, guns, transportation, outdoor clothing, camping equipment, lodging, ammunition, food, guides' fees, processing, taxidermy, and fuel amount to millions of dollars annually.

Hunting supports the economy, provides recreation, and keeps us in touch with our heritage. Little wonder it has endured so many years. Now let's address the biggest benefit of all—good eating!

To most enjoy your venison, you must consider several things. Field dressing and cleanliness must be attended to immediately after the kill. The meat should not be exposed to warm temperatures. Venison, as well as all large game, must cool for at least 36 hours before cooking. Hang your venison in a cool, dark place, protected from insects, with the chest cavity propped open. Both freezing and hanging will age your kill, breaking down the fibers and tenderizing the meat.

The environment, age, and feeding habits of the white-tailed deer greatly affect the flavor of the meat. Deer taken from predominantly forested terrain where the animals have subsisted on browse will be generally stronger in flavor than those taken from farm areas where the deer graze on pasture grasses, apples, and corn. Adjustments in cooking must be made for the age of the animal as well. Determining the age of a deer is difficult, but the most effective way to estimate it is to examine the teeth. Inspect the rear teeth and look for missing teeth or signs of wear on the molars. Deer have a set of "baby teeth" called milk teeth. At one year, a deer will have his first set of milk teeth. At age one and one-half, the first three milk teeth will be worn, but the last three will be sharp and new permanent teeth. At age two, the front teeth will be new, while the permanent teeth in the back will already be showing signs of wear. After three to three and one-half years, all permanent teeth will be wearing, and deer of this age will require special preparation to tenderize the meat well.

A few guidelines to follow after determining the approximate age of your deer are:

Type A Meat

1. Prepare young, corn-fed deer according to your favorite beef recipes.

2. Prepare young mountain-dwelling deer carefully using my recipes for steaks, rare meat, or in roasts.

3. Prepare tender meat using recipes calling for fast, open heat, such as frying, broiling, or pan frying.

Type B Meat

1. Prepare older meat using slower, moister cooking, such as baking in a covered dish, pot roasting, slow cooker methods.

2. Avoid cooking older, browse-fed animals with the bone or any fat, as these tend to be strong. Trim all older meat well to eliminate this strong taste. In other words, if your meat fits this description and you do not like the "wild" taste of game, do not use chops, rib steaks, rib roasts, or roasts with the bone in. Consider this when giving your butcher instructions.

Every year, then, your instructions to the butcher will be different depending upon the size, age, and location of your kill.

The recipes in this book suitable to use in preparing older, tougher, and stronger meat are indicated as "Type B" throughout.

After analyzing the diet of your deer and its age, you need to give some thought to butchering, even if you plan to have it done professionally. Steaks, chops, and rack roasts can be cut from the ribs or loin and prepared following the recipes in this book. Use the scraps from the extremities, shoulder, and haunch for stew meat or ground meat. Add pork to the ground meat for moistness and flavor, if desired. One part pork to three parts venison is a good proportion to follow.

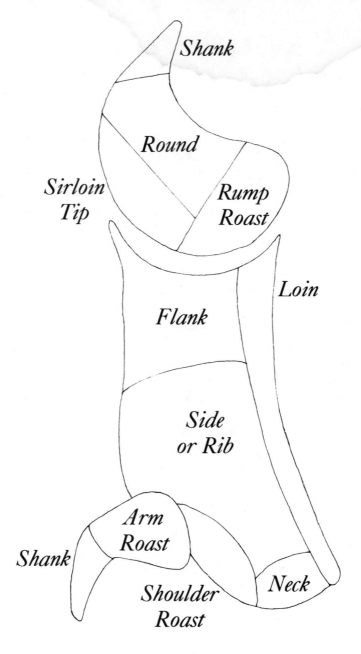

Shank

Round

Sirloin Tip

Rump Roast

Loin

Flank

Side or Rib

Arm Roast

Shank

Shoulder Roast

Neck

FIELD DRESSING
LARGE GAME

Field dressing is important to preserve the quality of the meat. Field dress your game as soon as possible after the kill. All large animals should be eviscerated, skinned, and dried as soon as possible. Evisceration is so important because it begins the cooling process and preserves the quality and taste of the meat.

With the animal on its back, block up the body to keep it supported and steady. Make first cut into animal in center of belly between the hind legs. Cut up to the tip of breastbone (between front legs) and down to anus. After the skin has been opened and pulled back, you are ready to make an incision into the body cavity. Follow the path of original cut right into and through body flesh. Pull carcass open and split the pelvis into two pieces. Tip the split-opened animal on its side and empty it of all internal organs. Remove the windpipe, heart, lungs, paunch, and lower organs.

When cutting around the anus, it is advisable to tie off the anus with some twine before pulling it through the pelvis for removal. Do not let this part of the animal touch any of the meat for fear of contamination, and do not drag it over meat when removing skin in this area.

Open the breastbone by cutting along the centerline with a heavy knife or hatchet. Deer can be opened with a knife. Larger animals require heavier instruments. Save the liver and heart. Prop the body cavity open to speed cooling. Wipe out the body cavity with clean material (grass or toweling, for example).

Save the skinning of your animal for home or base camp. If you are taking your animal to a butcher, he will skin it for you, though butchering your own game is not that difficult and holds tremendous rewards. But if you feel that you just can't do it, or time does not permit, then at least skin it yourself. Skinning should be done as soon as possible anyway, to cool the meat down. By doing it yourself you can assure that there will be no stray hair in the finished product. The skin is also much easier to remove immediately than after the animal has cooled down. Once the skin has been removed, wipe the carcass down using clean towels and fresh water until no hair remains. Being meticulous during this step will pay off everytime you dine on venison.

Storing Venison

When we purchase meat at the store, we expect it to be labeled as to the cut and quality, which determines what we do with it. You would never broil a piece of brisket, for example. We pay more for a Prime cut because it will be more tender than a Choice quality, which refers to the aging. Give your game the same consideration that you expect at the super market. Instruct your butcher to label the packages as to the cut, or do it yourself as you process it.

Packaging is extremely important to the final product. A side of beef purchased from a butcher arrives ready for the freezer, tightly wrapped in heavy freezer-quality paper and labeled. Steaks, chops, rib roast, chuck roast, brisket, tenderloin, eye roast, sirloin, all indicate the cut, and that dictates the method of cooking. Add to that the approximate age, date, and type of meat, and you have a package that can be prepared successfully. We all know some pieces require moist heat while others are tender enough to be broiled or roasted. To simplify the explanation of the type of venison you are packaging, I recommend labeling the meat Type A or Type B. If in doubt, I usually cut off a small steak and fry it up while I'm wrapping the meat. Nothing like a taste test to know for sure.

So, use a quality wrapping paper and label your packages giving the information discussed above. How many times have we all reached into the freezer and pulled out what my family calls "mystery meat"? It's frustrating trying to figure out what to do with it.

Perhaps the biggest enemy of frozen food is evaporation caused by self-defrost refrigerators. These come equipped with fans and heaters to melt the ice that builds up on freezer shelves, but they also draw moisture from any unsealed package causing freezer burn. If you are planning to keep any kind of meat for more than six weeks, I recommend encasing it in a layer of ice. This is simple and easy to do and increases the shelf life several months. Simply freeze the meat as usual, then remove from freezer and unwrap. Run the frozen meat under a thin stream of cold water, coating all surfaces. As the water hits the frozen meat, it will turn into ice, thus encasing the meat in a "block of ice." Refreeze, and repeat this process several times until the "block of ice" is several layers thick and will effectively seal all surfaces. Rewrap and store up to nine to ten months with no loss of flavor.

EASY BARBECUED VENISON
Types A-B

1 16 oz. can peaches with juice

1 14 oz. bottle ketchup

3-pound venison roast

Blend first two ingredients in blender or food processor until smooth. Pour over meat. Bake covered in a Dutch oven at 200° for a minimum of one hour per pound. Can also be cooked in a slow cooker set on low for five to six hours, depending on the size of the roast.

Gauge cooking time according to the size of the meat. Allow about twice the time you would for beef, at half the cooking temperature. Slow simmering brings out the barbecued flavor.

Note: Start with this recipe, and its success will motivate you to cook more game. This is an excellent barbecue sauce and almost too easy to believe. Use it on pork, chicken, or beef. It makes excellent barbecued spareribs and barbecued chicken.

Serves 4

VENISONBRATEN
Types A-B

Marinade
2 cups water
1 cup red wine vinegar
1/2 cup cider vinegar
2 medium onions, sliced
1/2 cup brown sugar
4 bay leaves
6 whole peppercorns
1/2 cup red Burgundy

4-to-6 pound venison
*   roast*
1 tablespoon cooking oil

Gravy
1 cup meat juices
1/2 pint sour cream
1/2 cup broken gingersnaps

Combine first seven ingredients in a saucepan; heat and stir to dissolve sugar. Add wine after heat is turned off. Cool. Pour over roast, and marinate four to seven days in refrigerator. Turn twice daily. In Dutch oven, brown meat in hot oil, turning to brown all sides, then lower heat to simmer. Pour strained marinade over roast and cook covered in Dutch oven on top of stove at lowest setting for two hours for a small roast, or up to three hours for larger pieces of meat. May also be cooked in the oven, covered, at 200° for three to five hours. Meat should flake apart with fork when done. For gravy, combine meat juices and sour cream over low heat. Add gingersnaps to thicken. Heat through.

Note: Hearty, well-seasoned German dish that goes well with buttered noodles on a cold winter night.

Serves 6

GRILLED ROSEMARY ROAST

Types A–B

3- to 5-pound venison roast
2 to 3 cloves of fresh garlic
1 tablespoon dried rosemary

salt and pepper to taste
1/4 cup butter
3 tablespoons Worcestershire Sauce

Spear roast with an ice pick or sharp knife in six or eight places. Cut each garlic clove into pieces and insert a piece into each hole. Rub surface with rosemary, salt and pepper. Get the charcoal going in a grill with a lid. Make a pan using several layers of heavy aluminum foil to catch the drippings and place on top of coals. Melt the butter and add the Worcestershire Sauce. Set roast on grill, and cover. Baste with butter mixture every fifteen to twenty minutes. Grill one hour or more, depending on size.

Serves 4–6

STEAK NORMANDE

Type A

*2 venison round steaks
    sliced ¹/₄ to ¹/₂ inch
    thick*
Dijon-style mustard
6 tablespoons butter
*2 cups sliced fresh mush-
    rooms*

*¹/₂ cup sliced green
    onions*
2 cloves garlic, crushed
2 teaspoons steak sauce
¹/₂ cup mushroom liqueur
¹/₂ cup cognac

Coat both sides of steaks with mustard and allow to stand at room temperature one hour. Melt three tablespoons of the butter and sauté the sliced mushrooms, stirring frequently. Remove mushrooms, set aside. Measure mushroom-butter liqueur left in pan. If more than one half cup, reduce by boiling for several minutes. Cook onions and garlic in remaining butter. Add steak sauce, mushrooms and liqueur. Bring liquid to a boil, reduce heat and add steaks, one at a time. Cook each steak three minutes per side. Place under broiler for one minute per side. Remove from pan immediately to heated platter. Place pan under broiler again just until juices return to a boil. Pour juices over steaks, and drizzle cognac over all. Ignite and serve immediately.

Serves 2

TENDERLOIN OF VENISON GRAND MARNIER

8 ounces Grand Marnier　　*2 whole tenderloins*
1 orange　　*3 tablespoons oil*

Place one half the Grand Marnier in a plastic bag. Slice one half the orange. Remove the zest from the other half and squeeze juice into the bag. Place tenderloins in the liqueur and cover with orange slices. Allow to marinate four to five hours.

Remove meat from the bag and discard marinade. Brush all surfaces of meat with oil. Place on a rack in an open pan. Preheat oven to 500°. Insert meat thermometer into thickest portion of largest loin. Place in oven and immediately reduce heat to 325°. Roast until internal temperature is 130°. Time will vary depending on size of the tenderloins.

To serve, slice at an angle, cover with Brown sauce (recipe follows) and garnish with more orange sections and fresh parsley, if desired.

Serves 4

BROWN SAUCE

6 tablespoons butter
2 slices onion
6 tablespoons flour

2¹/₂ cups beef stock
salt and pepper to taste

Heat the butter in a small heavy skillet over low heat until browned. Add and sauté the onion slices until light brown. Remove the onion and stir in the flour until well blended. Cook over low heat, stirring constantly, until flour is a deep mahogany brown. This takes fifteen to twenty minutes. Remove from heat. Gradually stir in the beef stock. Cook over low heat, stirring constantly, until thickened. Remove from heat and stir in the reserved Grand Marnier.

Make this sauce the day before the meal. It simplifies the preparation, and allows the sauce to ripen in flavor. Heat gently before serving.

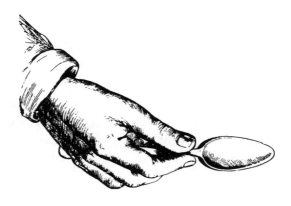

PAUL JUKES' VENISON STEAKS

Wyoming Valley outdoor writer and photographer Paul Jukes believes good grilled venison begins in the field. "Kitchen magicians often get into hot water when attempting to adapt everyday recipes for use with wild game. Nowhere is this more evident than in cooking venison. Proper field care is imperative for best results. For maximum yield, begin with a properly placed shot, preferrably in the heart/lung area. Once the animal is down, remove the internal organs as soon as possible, taking care not to puncture the intestines." Jukes also advises cutting the loin into large pieces, freezing and then cutting individual steaks when ready to grill.

1 whole venison loin,   *salt and pepper to taste*
    thawed
barbecue sauce

Cut steaks about one inch thick. Get the charcoal smoking hot and sear the steaks on both sides to seal in the juices. Lower the heat and cook for five minutes then turn. Grill another minute or two for medium rare, a little longer for medium well done steaks. Brush steaks with barbecue sauce last few minutes of cooking time. Salt and pepper to taste and serve immediately.

Note: Mr. Jukes is so right in his observation that venison cannot be treated like beef. Venison is not marbled with fat and cooks completely differently. A one-inch thick beef steak would need several more minutes cooking time than recommended here. I have learned to test venison for doneness by "feeling." After turning the steaks, begin to push on the surface every few seconds. You will be able to feel the flesh firming up as it cooks. With just a little practice, it is possible to catch your venison at just the exact doneness preferred.

Serves 6–8 depending on the size of the loin

VENISON HEART

1 fresh venison heart   *¹/₂ cup dry, red wine*
1 onion, sliced   *4 to 5 tablespoons butter*

Clean and rinse heart. Cut into strips one inch by three or four inches. Place in a bowl and cover with the onion slices. Pour wine over and allow to stand at room temperature thirty to forty minutes. Melt butter in a heavy skillet. Over medium heat, sauté strips of heart two to three minutes per side. Serve immediately.

Serves 2–4

BAKED VENISON LIVER

¹/₄ cup cornstarch
3 tablespoons flour
1 fresh venison liver
¹/₂ pound hickory smoked
  bacon, sliced thinly

1 cup grated raw carrot
1 can tomato soup
1 teaspoon sweet basil
dash garlic powder
dash paprika for garnish

Combine cornstarch and flour. Cut liver into serving-size pieces and dredge in flour mixture. Fry bacon; drain, crumble and set aside. Brown liver in bacon fat three minutes on each side. Liver will be "rare" at this point. Remove liver from pan. Add carrot and soup to pan, stirring constantly. Simmer five minutes. Place liver in baking dish and top with tomato soup mixture. Sprinkle with basil and garlic powder. Bake at 350° thirty to thirty-five minutes. Garnish with crumbled bacon and paprika.

Note: Even the non-liver eater in the family will like this.

Serves 6

VICTORY VENISON LIVER WITH ONIONS

¹/₄ cup shortening
2 Bermuda onions, sliced
1 green pepper, sliced into
  rings
1 cup sliced fresh mush-
  rooms, cooked
¹/₂ cup flour
1 fresh venison liver

Melt shortening in a large skillet and add onion slices and green pepper rings. Cook on medium heat until onions are transparent and pepper rings are crisp but tender. Add mushrooms and heat through. Push vegetables aside.

While onions and peppers are cooking, cut liver into half-inch slices and dredge in the flour. Increase heat and quickly fry liver slices just to brown surface. Turn slices and cover with vegetables. Reduce heat and cook one to two minutes more. Liver is best if slightly pink in the center. Serve immediately.

Note: This is the traditional Victory Dinner after a successful day afield in Paul Jukes' home.

Serves 4

RUTH STEVENSON'S CHINESE PEPPER STEAK

Type A

2 large onions, sliced
2 cups fresh mushrooms, sliced thinly
1 or 2 sliced red and green peppers
1 clove garlic, crushed
1/4 cup peanut oil
1 1/2 pounds venison tenderloin, cut in strips

1/4 cup soy sauce
1/2 cup beef bouillon
1/2 cup cold water
1/2 teaspoon black pepper
1/2 teaspoon honey
1 teaspoon ground ginger
1 tablespoon cornstarch

Sauté the onions, mushrooms, peppers and garlic in the peanut oil until vegetables are crisp. Remove vegetables from the wok or pan and add venison. Brown lightly and remove. Add all other ingredients to pan and cook over medium heat until smooth sauce is just under a boil. Return vegetables and meat to pan and heat through. Serve over rice.

Serves 4–6

VENISON ORIENTAL
Type A

Soy Marinade
1 cup oil
³/₄ cup soy sauce
1 teaspoon dry mustard
2 teaspoons Worcestershire
  Sauce

1 pound venison steak
2 tablespoons oil

1 cup fresh broccoli
1 medium onion, sliced
1 cup fresh mushrooms,
  sliced
1 small stalk celery
  cabbage, sliced thin
¹/₂ cup fresh green beans
1 red or green pepper,
  julienned

Combine marinade ingredients in a jar and shake or combine in a blender. Pour over steak in a shallow dish or sealable plastic bag. Let stand overnight or 36 hours. Turn once.

Remove steaks from marinade and cut into strips. Sauté quickly in oil in large skillet or wok, a few pieces at a time. Push pieces to the side as you turn them. When all steak has been sautéed, remove from pan.

Sauté fresh vegetables until crisp-tender (about 4–6 minutes). Cover pan and steam vegetables 2–3 minutes more. Remove lid and return meat to wok or pan. Stir meat and vegetables another 2–3 minutes to reheat meat. Add marinade to the pan to taste (3–4 tablespoons) and stir well. Serve over rice or Chinese noodles.

This is the recipe that gave me confidence in the preparation of game. My husband and son didn't know it was venison, and a dinner guest came back the next morning for the recipe. This is easy to prepare and works equally well with beef and pork. Use a bag of frozen Oriental vegetables if you must to shorten preparation time, or vary the vegetable combination to taste.

Serves 4

PAUL JUKES' SHAVED VENISON SAUTÉ

Type A

1 partially frozen 2 to 3 pound venison steak
1/2 cup butter
2 cups fresh mushrooms, sliced

3 tablespoons steak sauce
2 cups light cream
3 to 4 tablespoons flour
salt and pepper to taste

With a sharp knife shave paper thin slices from the partially frozen steak. Melt half the butter in a skillet over low heat. Sauté venison slices carefully until thawed and slightly pink, about medium rare. Remove to a heated platter and continue cooking until all slices have been sautéed. After all meat has been cooked, add the mushrooms and remaining butter to the pan and cook five to six minutes, stirring occasionally. Add the steak sauce and salt and pepper to taste.

Blend the flour and cream and add slowly to the mushrooms, continuing to cook until sauce thickens. Ladle sauce over hot venison shavings and serve immediately.

Serves 2–3

INDIAN VENISON

Type B

4-to-6 pound venison roast   *1 cup maple syrup*

Marinate the roast in the syrup at room temperature for four hours. Cover and refrigerate for two days, turning twice a day. Roast in syrup covered in slow oven (250°) for three hours or until tender.

This is a traditional recipe. Native Americans, who loved maple sugar and maple syrup, enjoyed their venison exactly this way. Champlain found them using this method in the seventeenth century. Their children loved to trickle the hot golden syrup onto the snow and eat it, as New England children do to this day. Easy.

Serves 4–6

VENISON POT PIE
Type B

*1 venison roast (1 to 3
    pounds)*
1 teaspoon parsley
1 teaspoon oregano
*16 oz. pot pie noodles, or
    homemade noodles, or
    any large, wide egg
    noodle*

*2 large potatoes, peeled
    and diced*
1 onion, chopped coarsely
1 can beef bouillon

Brown roast on all sides in oil in heavy pot. Cover with one to two quarts of water, add parsley, oregano, and salt and pepper to taste. Simmer, uncovered, two to three hours. Remove meat from the pot, cool, trim, and cut into bite-sized pieces. Add remaining ingredients to water in the pot and simmer until noodles are cooked. Add the meat and adjust seasonings to taste.

Note: This is a Pennsylvania Dutch dish that is usually served with a sweet and a sour side dish. Try pepper cabbage and sour green beans for the sour, and applebutter or cottage cheese for the sweet, for an authentic Pennsylvania Dutch supper. Do try the homemade noodles; they really are easy and well worth the extra effort, and you'll find the recipe for them in the Down Home section of this book.

Serves 4

VENISON AU NATUREL

Type A

*1 large onion
1 cup hearty red wine
Venison steaks (1 to 2
   pounds)*

*4 tablespoons butter or
   margarine (one-half
   stick)*

Cover fresh or frozen steaks with red wine and a large strong onion, sliced. Allow to marinate four to six hours. Cook quickly in melted butter with the wine-soaked onions. Reserve wine. Remove steaks to heated platter. Return marinade to pan and stir until just boiling. Pour over steaks and serve.

Note: This is my son's special recipe. He whips these up in a flash and likes his rare. I find venison difficult to judge in degrees of doneness. It turns very quickly from rare to well-done. If you want rare steaks, give these your undivided attention. A good rule-of-thumb for half-inch steaks is one and one-half to two minutes per side for rare. Easy.

Serves 4

BLACK DIAMOND STEAKS

Type A

Marinade
1 cup oil
1 cup hearty red wine
1 onion, chopped
*¼ cup Dijon-style
    mustard*
½ teaspoon oregano
¼ teaspoon basil
1 clove garlic, crushed

4 to 6 venison steaks

Blend all marinade ingredients in the blender, food processor, or with a mixer. Cover steaks with the marinade. Turn twice a day for four to six days. To cook, grill or broil to desired doneness. These are best served medium-rare.

Note: This is an exceptionally rich, delicious steak. Made with beef tenderloin, it's festive and elegant. Serve with a green salad. Easy.

Serves 4

VENISON STEAK EXTRAORDINAIRE

Type A

½ cup olive oil
¼ cup white wine vinegar
6 to 8 boneless slices of
   venison, one-half-inch
   thick
2 to 4 tablespoons
   additional oil for
   frying

2 cups bread
   stuffing, prepared
1 cup spaghetti sauce
12 oz. Mozzarella cheese,
   sliced
¼ cup grated Parmesan
   cheese

Mix olive oil and vinegar. Pour over steaks and allow to marinate four to six hours. Remove from marinade, and sauté in medium hot skillet in a little olive oil. Add olive oil as necessary to keep steaks from sticking. Remove browned steaks to foil covered cooky sheet. Place a pat (about a quarter cup) of stuffing on top of each steak and flatten it. Cover stuffing with one to two tablespoons of spaghetti sauce, and top with a slice of Mozzarella. Sprinkle with Parmesan cheese. Cover loosely with foil, and bake at 300° for one hour.

Note: These steaks are beautiful looking and really delicious. Try serving with an elegant artichoke salad and peas with rice. This recipe is delicious with beef round steaks, also.

Prepared stuffing mix can be substituted for homemade, and a small jar of Italian tomato sauce or marinara sauce serves well in place of "from scratch" spaghetti sauce.

VENISON FINGERS
Type A

Marinade
½ cup olive oil
¼ cup red wine vinegar
2 teaspoons fresh oregano
　or 1 teaspoon dried
2 teaspoons fresh basil or
　1 teaspoon dried
½ teaspoon salt
1 garlic clove, crushed

1 pound venison steaks
1 cup unseasoned cracker-
　meal
¼ cup olive oil
4 tablespoons margarine
　(one-half stick)—butter
　will burn too easily

Combine oil, vinegar, garlic, and seasonings for marinade. Cut steaks into finger-sized strips. Put in a single layer in a glass dish or in a sealable bag, and cover with marinade. Marinate overnight or for two to four days. (The longer the marinating time, the less wild the flavor.) Remove meat and dredge in cracker-meal without draining. The marinade will make the cracker-meal stick well! Pat the meal firmly into meat on all sides. Bring olive oil and margarine to 325° (medium heat) in an electric frying pan. Sauté strips until golden. Drain on paper towels. Serve hot as an appetizer, if desired.

Note: I use the electric frying pan for this, because I can control the heat. You may use any sort of skillet, as long as you can keep a consistent low temperature.

To the uninitiated, this passes for very tasty veal.

Serves 4 as an entrée
Serves 6–8 as an appetizer

VENISON SCALLOPINI

Types A-B

¹/₂ cup olive oil
¹/₄ cup dry white wine
1 garlic clove, crushed
1 pound boneless venison steak, trimmed and cut
¹/₂ cup flour
1 teaspoon paprika

2 cups prepared spaghetti sauce, or your own
1 8 oz. can button mushrooms
1 cup fresh mushrooms, sliced very thin
3 tablespoons parsley

Combine half the olive oil, the wine, and garlic to make a marinade. Mix well, pour it over prepared meat, and let stand at room temperature two to three hours. Place flour and paprika in paper bag. Shake to mix. Remove meat from marinade and pat dry. Pound on both sides to tenderize. Drop into bag of flour, and shake to coat. Brown floured meat in remaining quarter cup of olive oil. Remove meat from skillet and drain. Arrange in a single layer in large frying pan. Pour spaghetti sauce over meat, and simmer covered for one hour. Fifteen minutes before serving, add mushrooms and parsley. Cover frying pan and cook 15 minutes more. Serve immediately.

Note: This scallopini can be cooked in half the time using a pressure cooker instead of the electric fry pan. 10–12 minutes in the pressure cooker will produce tender, delectable meat.

Serves 4

VENISON PARMESAN
Types A-B

Marinade
2/3 cup oil
1/4 cup vinegar
2 tablespoons water
2 tablespoons onion,
   finely grated
1 clove garlic, minced
1/2 teaspoon oregano
1/2 teaspoon dried red bell
   pepper
1/4 teaspoon basil
1/4 teaspoon sugar
1/4 teaspoon salt

4 to 6 venison steaks
2 cups or more Italian
   breadcrumbs
3 eggs, well beaten
4 oz. butter or margarine
   (one stick)
1/2 cup olive oil
1 cup tomato puree or
   spaghetti sauce
1 pound Mozzarella
   cheese, sliced
1/4 cup grated Parmesan
   cheese

Mix marinade in a jar and shake to mix well. Pour over steaks to cover. (I use a plastic sealable bag.) Marinate two to seven days, turning occasionally. The longer the marination, the milder the venison flavor and the spicier the result.

Dredge steaks in bread crumbs while still wet with marinade. Dip into beaten egg and then into bread crumbs again. Can be prepared up to this point hours ahead. Cover and refrigerate until cooking time.

Melt margarine in electric frying pan. Add the olive oil and heat to 350°. Stir to combine. Sauté steaks until golden brown on both sides. Drain on paper toweling. Place a generous tablespoon of tomato puree on top of each steak and then a slice of Mozzarella. Sprinkle with grated Parmesan cheese. Bake on a cooky sheet at 350° for 15 minutes. Run under the broiler to brown cheese.

Serve to rounds of applause. This entrée looks beautiful on a platter with spaghetti. Pass the remaining sauce and more grated cheese.

Note: Of course you can make your own bread crumbs with stale bread in the blender or food processor. For flavored crumbs, add ½ teaspoon oregano, ¼ teaspoon basil, and a dash of garlic powder if desired.

To make this recipe fast and easy, substitute prepared Italian salad dressing mix for the marinade, according to package directions.

Serves 4

JIM VANCE'S "CORNED BEEF-STYLE" VENISON

If you were fortunate enough to have bagged a large game animal that yields a great deal of meat, this recipe will give you some variety in the preparation and taste. Making a 'Corned Beef-type' roast is fun and interesting. This preparation works well for all large game animals.

4 to 6 pound boneless roast (moose, caribou, elk, venison)
3 bay leaves, crushed
1 teaspoon cloves
1 teaspoon mace
1 teaspoon allspice
1/2 teaspoon peppercorns, crushed

4 tablespoons brown sugar
1 tablespoon salt
1 tablespoon pepper
1/2 pound coarse salt
1 teaspoon garlic powder

Clean and trim roast. Mix dry ingredients and rub spices into meat on all sides. Place roast and extra spices in a large plastic freezer bag. Pat spices into the roast again, shaking bag to distribute extra spices. Refrigerate seven days, turning and rubbing the spices into the meat each day. After the first day, roast will be marinating in its own juices.

On the seventh day, rinse under cold water and discard spices. Tie roast securely several times with twine at three- to four-inch intervals to prevent it from separating. Place roast in a large kettle and cover with water. Bring to a boil and reduce heat. Simmer covered five hours. Remove from heat, drain and cool. Wrap the meat in foil, place between two boards and weight down. Cutting boards work well for this, and a pot of stew or soup makes a good weight. Refrigerate twelve hours.

Prepare as you would corned beef. Simmer in water with potatoes and cabbage or slice thinly against the grain and serve in sandwiches. This product will be slightly drier than beef, as is always the case for wild game with its low fat content.

BARBECUED TENDERLOIN

Type A

1 whole venison tender-
loin
³/₄ cup barbecue sauce

salt and papper to taste

Fillet the loin strips from alongside the backbone of your deer. Cut each tenderloin in half. Double a sheet of aluminum foil, lay the fillet on the top, season with salt and pepper to taste and cover with barbecue sauce (see pages 13, 40, 46, or your own favorite). Wrap tightly and lay directly on coals. After one half hour turn and cook for another thirty-five to forty minutes. Slice and serve immediately.

Serves 4

OLD FASHIONED BARBECUE
Type B

1 pound venison, any cut
1 cup water
1 teaspoon oregano
2 tablespoons butter

1 16 oz. bottle hot *ketchup*
Sweet pickle relish, optional

Place meat in a slow cooker. Add water, oregano, and salt to taste. Simmer covered on medium heat until meat falls apart (one and one-half to two hours), or approximately one and one-half hours per pound. Remove meat with slotted spoon; discard broth. Allow to cool. Shred meat, discarding fat and bones. Melt butter in saucepan. Add ketchup and blend. Stir in shredded meat and heat through.

We like this served on buttered, toasted buns heaped with sweet pickle relish.

Note: This recipe takes care of any cuts of game you don't like or don't know what to do with. I used shoulder steaks for this one year. The shoulder steaks were bony, and we didn't care for them at all, so into the slow cooker they went. Easy.

Serves 4

COCKTAIL MEATBALLS

Types A-B

1 pound ground venison
1 pound fresh bulk sausage
1 cup bread crumbs
4 eggs
1/2 cup ketchup
1/2 onion, grated
1/2 cup grated Parmesan cheese

1/3 cup sugar
1 or 2 dashes Worcestershire sauce
1 teaspoon oregano
1 teaspoon basil
1 teaspoon crushed fennel seed
1 teaspoon nutmeg
2 quarts spaghetti sauce

Can be used as an appetizer or buffet dish. Combine all ingredients except spaghetti sauce in large bowl. Work through with the hands or a large wooden spoon until well blended. Bring spaghetti sauce to gentle boil in large heavy pot. Roll meat mixture into small meatballs, and drop them into sauce. Shake pot occasionally, but do not stir. Allow to simmer one-half hour. This method makes a hearty sauce, as the juices from the meatballs cook into it, and the meatballs themselves are very tender and soft. Eliminating the browning in oil reduces calories and cuts the preparation time in half. Should meatballs feel too soft as you form them, add a little more bread crumbs.

Note: This is a traditional dish on our Christmas day buffet table.

Serves 6–8

DIRECTIONS FOR MAKING VENISON SAUSAGE

Meat

1. Trim fat and gristle off carefully, as it would affect the taste of your finished product.
2. Partially frozen meat will grind more easily than cool meat.
3. In a food grinder, run some pork fat through first to grease the worm. The grinder can be cleaned easily if some bread is run through at the last.
4. It shortens the process to purchase loose sausage already ground at the market to add to your venison.

Casing

1. Purchase a tub of casings at your local market or provision plant.
2. Wash casings by threading one end over a faucet and holding while running warm water through them. Cut around or repair any tears or holes by tying them off.
3. Cut into two- to three-foot lengths.
4. Soak in warm water for an hour.
5. Remove one length of casing at a time, and extract water by holding one end with the thumb and forefinger, and then pulling the length of casing through the fingers, squeezing as it passes between them.

Filling the Casing

1. Put the stuffing horn on your food grinder.

2. Thread one end of casing onto the horn, and gradually push all of casing on, leaving only a two-inch length hanging.

3. Tie a knot in the hanging end to close the casing for stuffing.

4. Feed sausage into horn as you hold casing on horn. Do not allow any casing to come off the horn until the two-inch length is firm and full.

5. As you feed meat through, allow the casing to unroll slowly, making sure it is filled uniformly.

6. Stop filling occasionally to check uniformity, and pierce any air bubbles with a needle.

7. Sausage should just fill casing, not stretch it. Stretching the casing may cause the casing to burst during cooking.

8. To finish filling last of casing, remove horn and casing from grinder, and poke remaining sausage in the horn into the casing with the handle of a wooden spoon. Tie to close.

Repeat this process with each length of casing until you have used all your venison sausage.

Sausage should be dried on a rack to allow the casings to dry. This may be done in a refrigerator or on a rack in a cool room. Dry 12 to 24 hours.

Note: To make link sausage, cut two lengths of cased sausage about two feet long. Hold the sausage parallel and twist to join ends. About four inches from the joined end, squeeze both pieces to make an indentation in the casing. Lay one piece on top of the other, and again twist to join. You now have one double link. To form the next, bring one length of sausage up and through the space between the first links. Pull through and lay flat again alongside the other piece. Squeeze indentations four inches further down, and repeat twisting and pulling through the whole of the preceding link. This makes a very pleasing display of your homemade venison sausage, which looks lovely on a platter.

This is the authentic link sausage that will not come apart during cooking. I learned this procedure in my father's butcher shop.

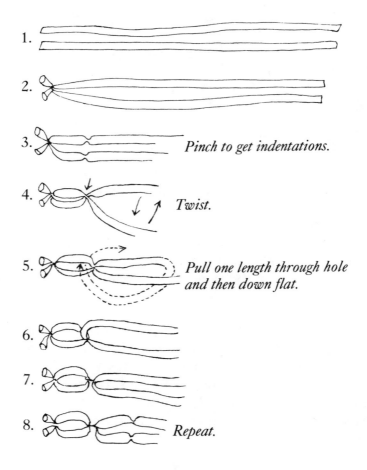

1.

2.

3. *Pinch to get indentations.*

4. *Twist.*

5. *Pull one length through hole and then down flat.*

6.

7.

8. *Repeat.*

MILD SAUSAGE
Types A-B

This recipe is for smaller amounts of sausage.

5 pounds lean venison,
ground
2 pounds pork, ground
5 tablespoons sage
2 tablespoons salt
2 tablespoons
monosodium glutamate

2 tablespoons cayenne
pepper
1 onion (medium)
3 tablespoons lemon juice

Cut onion into quarters and blend in blender or process with steel blade in food processor. Combine meats and spices, and add the onion and lemon juice. May be put into casings or used as bulk sausage.

Note: This is a mild sausage good for use at the breakfast table. One pound will serve four people.

ITALIAN VENISON SAUSAGE NUMBER ONE

Types A-B

2 oz. salt
2 oz. monosodium
  glutamate
2 oz. paprika
1 oz. cayenne pepper

¹/₂ oz. black pepper
¹/₂ oz. sage
¹/₂ oz. fennel seed,
  crushed
¹/₂ oz. oregano

Mix these spices into every ten pounds of ground venison/pork mixture. Wrap and freeze. May be stuffed into casings. One pound will serve four.

ITALIAN VENISON SAUSAGE NUMBER TWO

Types A-B

This is another version of Italian Sausage using smaller amounts.

5 pounds lean venison,
  ground
2 pounds pork, ground
5 tablespoons sage

4 tablespoons fennel seed,
  crushed
3 tablespoons oregano
3 tablespoons basil

3 *tablespoons paprika*
2 *tablespoons salt*
2 *tablespoons*
  monosodium glutamate
2 *teaspoons black pepper*

2 *teaspoons cayenne*
  pepper
1 *teaspoon garlic powder,*
  or to taste

Add all seasonings to ground meat, and mix as you would for a meatloaf. Can be put in casings if desired. Sausage is moist and spicy. To make Hot Sausage, add red pepper sauce and dried red pepper to this recipe. One pound of recipe should serve four.

Note: This sausage is good in soup recipes calling for sausage. (I offer several—look for Harvest Soup.) It is excellent in Mexican dishes, or in place of hamburger.

Cooking Suggestions

1. Cook venison Italian sausage in tomato juice, tomato puree, or spaghetti sauce. Bring the liquid of your choice to a boil, and gently simmer pierced sausages until sausage juices run clear. The sausage enhances the sauce, and the sauce livens up the sausage.
2. Poach gently in Pheasant Stock (page 104). Do not pierce sausage, unless you want the sausage to flavor the broth. Resulting broth may be used as soup base.
3. Poach gently in Beef Bouillon. Pierce sausage and serve broth as consommé for a first course. Float parsley on top for garnish.
4. Poach in wine or beer. Do not pierce sausage. Discard liquid.

Freeze sausage uncooked for best results.

BOB BERQUIST'S VENISON SAUSAGE

Bob Berquist, an excellent archer, meatcutter, banker, shares his expertise on the professional preparation of two kinds of venison sausage. Bob advises, "When cutting up the meat, do it with care. Be sure to remove the tallow (fat) from the deer and the fatty gland located in the middle of each hind quarter. To further preserve the flavor, cut the meat from the bone, rather than cut through the bones with a meat saw. This keeps the bone marrow from being spread throughout the meat. When grinding the meat for sausage, it is best to use a sausage plate on the grinder. This will give the meat a coarse consistency like that of commercially made sausage."

Bob doesn't add pork to venison because he says this automatically shortens the meat's freezer life and changes the taste of the meat. He also provides us with a recipe for pure venison sausage.

4 pounds ground venison
4 pounds ground beef
3 oz. black pepper

1/2 oz. paprika
1 1/4 oz. crushed red pepper

Wet the hands with water and combine the two meats with your hands. When the meats have been mixed thoroughly, add the spices and rewet the hands. Wet hands prevent the meat from sticking to them as much as it normally would.

Bob says, "I hate to leave anything to chance, so I always test each batch of sausage by frying up a few patties immediately. That's half the fun of making sausage at home!" This batch was great; not too hot with spices, yet tangy enough to have your taste buds appreciate the fact that red peppers were included in the ingredients.

This recipe and the following sausage variation came from Charlie Burchfield's column, "Outdoors Today" in the *Courier-Express*, DuBois, Pennsylvania. Charlie and Bob, both successful hunters, enjoy this sausage-making ritual each year.

PURE VENISON SAUSAGE

8 pounds ground venison
1 oz. black pepper

¹/₂ oz. paprika
¹/₄–¹/₃ oz. crushed red pepper

Proceed exactly as for Bob's original recipe. He tells us, "When making sausage with pure venison, you have to reduce the quantity of spices somewhat. Since there is very little fat content to pure venison, a greater percentage of the spices remain in the meat, rather than fry off with the grease."

Note: This recipe is most useful for those on restricted diets, for it contains very little fat and cholesterol.

49

NEW ORLEANS RED BEANS AND RICE

1 pound dried red kidney beans (two cups)
2 ham hocks
1/2 pound Italian venison sausage
2 1/2 quarts water

3 cloves garlic
salt and pepper to taste
1 teaspoon chili powder or "Creole Seasoning" (available in cooking shops)
2 cups cooked long grain rice

Wash beans and pick over. Soak overnight in a quart of water. Add another one and a half quarts water to the beans and place in a slow cooker. Trim all fat or skin off the ham hocks. Add whole ham hocks to the beans and simmer four to five hours or until meat is falling off the bone and beans are tender. Remove hocks from the pot and allow to cool. Cut the sausage into small pieces and add to beans. Add the remaining ingredients and simmer another hour. Remove the meat from the ham hocks and add to the pot. Cook until beans can be mashed into the stew, and stew is very thick. Serve over cooked hot rice.

Note: An all-time favorite, I always include this on a buffet table. It's typical Louisiana poor folk's fare—the South's answer to Italian pasta, and just as good.

Serves 6

SAUSAGE-STUFFED PEPPERS

8 medium size bell peppers
1 pound venison sausage
1 1/2 cups cooked rice
1 egg

2 tablespoons dried parsley
1/4 cup grated romano cheese
salt and pepper to taste
2 cups spaghetti sauce

Wash, cut off tops and clean out peppers. Sauté sausage and set aside to cool. Mix rice with the egg, parsley, cheese, salt and pepper. Drain any fat off the sausage and add sausage to mixture. Blend in one half cup of the spaghetti sauce. Mix well and stuff each pepper with filling. Place in a baking pan and pour remaining sauce over the peppers. Sauce should cover bottom of pan. Bake at 350° covered for thirty minutes. Baste each pepper with sauce and bake an additional fifteen to twenty minutes uncovered.

Serves 4–6

AUTHENTIC CHILI
Type B

1 pound venison, any cut (although you should have shredded meat for "authentic" chili)
1 teaspoon oregano
1 onion, chopped
2 tablespoons oil
1 20 oz. can Italian tomatoes, with juice
1 16 oz. can red kidney beans

1 6 oz. can tomato paste
2 tablespoons chili powder
1 teaspoon cumin
1 teaspoon fennel
1 teaspoon red pepper flakes
Red pepper sauce to taste.

Place meat in a slow cooker. Add water to half cover, and the oregano. Simmer covered on medium setting until meat flakes and falls apart (approximately one hour per pound). Remove meat with slotted spoon, and allow to cool. Reserve broth. Shred meat, discarding fat and bones. Sauté onion in oil until golden. Add all remaining ingredients, including broth, and bring to the simmer. Add meat, and simmer one-half hour. Adjust seasoning to taste.

Serves 4

VARIATIONS ON AUTHENTIC CHILI

1. Go Mexican. Add a can of ripe olives and a can of green chilies, chopped. Serve with corn chips, and pass the red pepper sauce.

2. Serve on a bed of rice for a complete meal.

3. Add two cans of mushrooms with juice and some chopped green pepper. (Drain the can of Italian tomatoes if you use the mushroom liquid in this way.)

4. Turn into a casserole, and top with Provolone, white American, or Mozzarella cheese. Drizzle a little corn syrup on top of cheese and bake until cheese melts.

5. Turn it into chili soup by adding a quart of beef broth and one more can of tomatoes, or a cup of tomato juice. Be creative—add mushrooms, alphabet noodles, rice—the possibilities are endless. Check the bottom shelf of the refrigerator. Leftover spaghetti cut up is a great addition.

The flavors in chili are always better if allowed to ripen. Make any of these several days prior to serving. Serve with a crusty French bread or a nice loaf of San Francisco's famous sourdough bread. (I've included my own favorite recipe for sourdough in the Down Home Section. Try it—sourdough could become a hobby.)

CHILI SOUP

Types A-B

1 pound venison, any cut
1 teaspoon oregano
1 20 oz. can Italian tomatoes, cut up, plus juice
1 16 oz. can kidney beans
1 cup fresh mushrooms or 1 8 oz. can mushrooms

1 6 oz. can tomato paste
1 envelope dry onion soup mix
1 teaspoon basil
1 teaspoon cumin
1 teaspoon Old Bay Seafood Seasoning

Prepare as for Authentic Chili, up through shredding the meat. After you have shredded the meat, add it with reserved liquid (approximately 1 quart) to all remaining ingredients in the slow cooker or large pot, and simmer one hour. This makes a delicious hearty one-dish meal. It is even better made a day in advance. Serve with crusty French bread and a salad.

Serves 4

MARY BEHLER'S TOMATO SAUCE

2 pounds ground venison
1 cup oil
1 large onion, minced
3 cloves garlic, minced
2 large cans (#2) Italian
  tomatoes
2 cans (6 oz.) tomato
  paste

1 can (1 lb.) tomato
  sauce
2 teaspoons salt
pepper to taste
1 teaspoon dried basil
1 cup sliced mushrooms
1/3 cup fresh parsley,
  minced

Brown the venison in the oil. Add the onion and cook two to three minutes. Add all remaining ingredients and simmer three hours, stirring occasionally. Serve with three pounds cooked spaghetti.

This is a hearty pasta dish for large groups—youngsters especially relish it. Prepare extra quantities of sauce and freeze in small portions; defrost in microwave for quick or impromptu meals.

Serves 8–10

MARY MALONE'S POSTASHODA

3 tablespoons olive oil
1 1/2 pounds ground veni-
  son
1 medium carrot sliced
2 stalks celery, chopped
1 small onion, chopped
3 cloves garlic
2 tablespoons minced
  fresh parsley

3 cans (8 oz.) tomato
  sauce
1/2 teaspoon ground cloves
1/3 teaspoon nutmeg
1/3 teaspoon allspice
1/4 teaspoon cayenne pep-
  per
salt to taste

Sauté venison in olive oil until lightly browned. Add remaining ingredients. Place in slow cooker at low setting for two hours. Serve over rice or pasta.

This is an unusual stew adapted from another of Aunt Mary's favorites.

WILD GAME TURKEY STUFFING

2 pounds ground venison
¹/₂ pound ground pork
6 eggs
1 teaspoon salt
¹/₂ teaspoon black pepper
1 stalk celery, chopped

¹/₂ cup raisins
¹/₂ cup sunflower seeds
  (optional)
¹/₄ cup grated sharp Italian cheese
1 small onion, chopped
1 large clove garlic, chopped

Combine pork and venison until mixed through. Add eggs and work until combined. Add all remaining ingredients. Stuff domestic or wild turkey and roast as usual.

Will stuff a small ten- to twelve-pound bird

NIG RANEY'S JOHNNY CAKE

2 cups corn meal
1 cup flour
2 teaspoons salt
1 teaspoon sugar
3 eggs
1/2 cup bacon drippings

1 can green jalapeño peppers, finely chopped
1 can cream-style corn
1 1/2 cups milk
1/2 pound ground venison

Mix dry ingredients together. Beat eggs and add bacon drippings, peppers, corn and milk. Stir to combine. Lightly sauté venison until just brown. Add to mixture. Heat iron skillet. Grease lightly and pour in batter. Bake until brown in 400° oven. Pour off excess grease.

Nig Raney is the Outdoor Editor of the *Brazorian News* in Lake Jackson, Texas, and a heck of a cook!

Serves four hungry Texans

OTHER LARGE GAME RECIPES

P repare caribou, moose, antelope, or elk the same as you would deer. Any recipe in the chapter on venison will work well. When in doubt as to an animal's age, always use a moist heat cooking method and marination, or *Type B* recipes. Young meats may be prepared as you would beef.

Elk may be aged from one to three weeks in 34° temperatures, according to taste. Antelope, caribou, and moose may be aged from three days to a week. Some connoisseurs of big game animals contend that freezing takes the place of aging, so you may want to experiment to see what works best for you.

To preserve moisture and flavor in the meat, wrap and freeze whole pieces of steak sections, and wait until just before cooking to slice into steaks. This gives you a fresh, juicy steak that is similar to freshly purchased sirloin of beef.

These other large animals are cut up the same way as deer or beef.

BEAR

A bear should be field dressed in the same manner as deer. Do not drag the animal if you want to save the hide. Because the bear is such a heavy animal, when setting out for a bear hunt you should be prepared with special equipment to field dress it. You will need a hoist and meat sacks, blankets, or canvas (and lots of ground pepper). Hang the animal and quarter the meat, storing it in sacks to keep it clean. Dry meat stays clean and bacteria-free, so make sure the meat is dry and free of flies. Should blowflies appear, rub pepper into surface, and dry area in the sun.

Bear can be aged from three to seven days. Aging permits the enzymes in the meat to tenderize it and improve the flavor. Fluctuation in temperature causes moisture to form on the meat, and moisture hastens the formation of bacteria, so whatever your plans for your meat, make sure the temperature is constant.

Meat from a young bear (one or two years old) is delicious. It can be prepared as you would pork using any moist heat recipe. Bear and sauerkraut, barbecued bear, bear "pigs-in-blankets," are all excellent choices. Slow cookers work well with bear. I include several recipes just to get you introduced to the sweet goodness of bear. After those, strike out on your own and experiment, using your favorite beef recipes or any of the venison recipes in this book.

ROAST OF BEAR

Marinade
*2 cups venison or beef
    broth*
1 large onion, sliced thin
$^1/_2$ teaspoon salt
*$^1/_2$ teaspoon monosodium
    glutamate*
$^1/_2$ teaspoon basil
$^1/_2$ teaspoon oregano
1 teaspoon paprika

1 4-to-6-pound bear roast

Place all ingredients in a deep bowl or bag to marinate. Turn roast at least twice, and marinate at least four hours. (A frozen roast can be marinated overnight in the refrigerator while thawing.) Add all ingredients to a slow cooker or Dutch oven, and cook on low setting one hour per pound, or four to six hours until tender. A tight-fitting lid is essential for this roast to tenderize the meat and enhance the flavor. Turn several times during cooking.

Serves 4

BEAR POT ROAST

Marinade
4 cups red wine
1 medium onion, sliced
2 bay leaves
1/2 teaspoon rosemary
4 to 6 black peppercorns,
  to taste (crushed)

3- to 4-pound bear roast
Oil for browning

Combine wine with all remaining ingredients except oil to make a marinade. Place roast in deep bowl, or in plastic bag, and pour marinade over. Turn every six hours to make sure all sides have been marinated. Refrigerate overnight. Before cooking, remove roast from marinade and pat dry. Heat oil in heavy Dutch oven. Brown meat lightly on all sides. Cover and bake in slow oven (250°) for one hour per pound. Baste with marinade several times.

Serves 4

HEARTY BEAR SOUP

2 large cans tomato juice (24 oz.)
1 large can stewed tomatoes (32 oz.)
1/2 cup barley
8 slices bacon
2 large stalks celery, diced
1 medium onion, chopped
2 large carrots, diced
1 medium potato, diced
1 pound ground bear meat

1 box frozen mixed vegetables (10 oz.)
1 box frozen corn (10 oz.)
1 teaspoon oregano
1 teaspoon basil
1 teaspoon paprika
1 teaspoon dried parsley
1/2 teaspoon garlic powder

In a large pot, bring tomato juice, stewed tomatoes and barley to a boil. Simmer. Sauté bacon in a frying pan until crisp. Remove from pan, cool, crumble and set aside. Sauté celery, onion, carrot, and potato in the bacon drippings until onion is translucent, and other vegetables are still crisp. Add vegetables to the simmering tomato mixture. Brown bear in the same fry pan. Add to the soup pot, stir to combine, and increase heat. Add remaining vegetables and seasonings, salt and pepper to taste. Bring to a boil, lower heat and simmer three to four minutes. Garnish each serving with the crisp bacon.

Serves 8–10

OLD ENGLISH BEAR SANDWICHES

Prepare roast as directed in Roast of Bear recipe. Proceed as follows: Slice cooled bear roast very thinly with electric knife or on meat slicer. Toast hard rolls under the broiler. Heap meat onto rolls and wrap in foil. Place in 375° oven five minutes to warm meat. To serve, hold roll sideways, and pour hot beef broth through meat. Serve with horseradish and hot peppers, if desired.

Note: Use your own beef broth or save the juice from a beef roast for this recipe and freeze. These natural beef juices give the finishing touch to this sandwich. Canned beef broth may also be used.

Serves 4

BARBECUED BEAR

1 16 oz. bottle ketchup   *3-to-4 pound bear roast*
1 10 oz. jar grape jelly

Combine the ketchup and jelly in a small sauce pan and heat until jelly dissolves. Pour over roast, and cook covered in a slow cooker or casserole in a slow oven (300°) for one hour per pound. Serve with the barbecue sauce from the cooking pot.

Note: Leftovers may be used for bear barbecue. Shred meat into sauce. Heat through. Serve on toasted hamburger rolls with pickle relish.

Serves 4

BEAR CHILI

2-to-3 pound bear roast
4 slices salt pork
2 large onions
1 16 oz. can kidney beans
1 6 oz. can tomato paste
1 tablespoon brown sugar

2 teaspoons chili powder
1 teaspoon seafood
   seasoning
1 teaspoon cumin
$1/2$ teaspoon oregano

Cook bear meat in covered pot with one cup water until cooked through and tender. Cook slowly. Remove meat from pot and discard water. Allow meat to cool and then shred into approximately two inch strands. Brown the salt pork in same pot. When pork is crisp, add the onions, and sauté until the onions are golden. Add remaining ingredients and one-half cup of water to rinse out tomato paste can. Heat through, and add the shredded bear meat. Adjust seasonings to taste. Garlic may be added if desired.

Note: This is an excellent recipe to use miscellaneous cuts of bear or scraps of meat. Cubes may also be used, or leftover roast bear.

To make Bear Chiliburgers, omit the half cup of water and the kidney beans. Mound on warm buns and serve as sandwiches.

BEAR STEW

3 slices bacon, diced
2 pounds bear cubes
4 medium onions,
   quartered
4 carrots, sliced
4 medium potatoes,
   quartered

1 package fresh or frozen
   peas
1 package fresh or frozen
   green beans
1 46 oz. can tomato juice
3 bay leaves

Brown bacon in heavy kettle or slow cooker. Add bear pieces, and brown on all sides. Add onions and sauté. Add all remaining ingredients, and cover and simmer one hour, or until flavors have mixed and meat and vegetables are tender.

Note: This recipe is equally good with venison, elk, or antelope.

Serves 4

BEAR MEAT JERKY

*1 pound or more bear
  meat*
1 quart warm water

2 to 3 cups liquid smoke
1 cup salt

Cut slices of meat (preferably hindquarter, or other tender cuts) one and one-quarter inches thick. Freeze slightly for easier handling. Cut each slice into quarter-inch thick strips. Soak in a mixture of water, salt, and liquid smoke for ten minutes. Drain well. Put directly on oven racks, being careful not to overlap strips. Sprinkle with pepper to taste. Turn oven to lowest setting, and bake three hours. Turn oven off, and let meat stand in oven until all heat has gone. Store in airtight jars.

Note: This recipe works equally well with venison.

67

ELK BURGUNDY
Type B

4-to-6 pound elk roast
1 cup red Burgundy
1 large onion, sliced
2 cloves garlic, minced

1/2 teaspoon rosemary
1/2 teaspoon thyme
6 peppercorns, crushed
Salt to taste

Combine all ingredients and allow to stand in refrigerator overnight. Turn meat and place with marinade in covered casserole. Bake at 300° for two hours, turning twice.

Serves 4–6

ELK ROAST
Type B

4-to-6 pound elk roast
1 12 oz. bottle beer

3 tablespoons steak sauce
6 peppercorns, crushed

Combine all ingredients and bake in a covered casserole at 250° for five hours. Baste frequently.

This is good with noodles and a green vegetable.

Serves 4–6

BEST ELK STEAKS EVER

Type A

1 3 oz. can green chilies, chopped and drained. Reserve liquid for marinade.
1 12 oz. bottle stout (or porter, ale, or beer)
1 to 2 pounds elk steaks

1 green pepper, chopped
4–6 green onions, thinly sliced
¹/₄ cup olive oil
Red pepper sauce to taste

Combine the green chili liquid and the stout for marinade. Marinate the steaks at room temperature four to six hours. Sauté the green pepper and onion in olive oil. Add green chilies and red pepper sauce to taste. Broil steaks to desired doneness. Top with green pepper mixture, and run steaks under the broiler until topping is sizzling.

Note: This recipe was inspired by the hot cuisine of our Southwest. It works well for all red meat.

Serves 4–6

ELK STROGANOFF

Types A-B

*1¹/₂ pounds elk round
  steak*
¹/₄ cup flour
¹/₄ cup pepper
¹/₄ cup olive oil
*2 teaspoons butter or
  margarine*

2 cups sliced mushrooms
1 medium onion, chopped
1 clove garlic (whole)
*2 cups venison or beef
  broth*
1 cup sour cream

Cut steaks into strips, then into pieces about two inches long. Dredge each strip in mixture of flour and pepper. Heat oil and butter or margarine in heavy skillet. Add onion and garlic clove. Stir until garlic is golden. Remove garlic clove, push onions to the side and brown floured meat on all sides. Remove meat from pan. Add mushrooms and sauté stirring constantly for ten minutes. Lower heat and add beef broth and sour cream. Stir until well blended. Return meat to pan and heat through (3–4 minutes).

Serve over noodles.

Note: Aunt Mag's homemade noodles make this dish extra-special (see Down Home section).

Serves 4

ROAST CARIBOU
Type B

3-to-4 pound caribou
   roast
1 cup hearty red wine
1 garlic clove, crushed
1 teaspoon meat
   tenderizer

1 cup whole berry
   cranberry sauce
1/4 cup honey
1 lemon, sliced

Marinate roast overnight in one-half cup wine and one-half cup water with the garlic clove. Apply tenderizer to outside of roast. Place in open roasting pan in 275° oven. Meanwhile, melt the cranberry sauce and honey in double boiler or over low heat. Remove from heat. Add the remaining half cup of wine. Stir to blend. Use this mixture to baste roast frequently. After two hours roasting time, top roast with sliced lemon and return to oven for two to three hours. Continue basting.

Serves 4–6

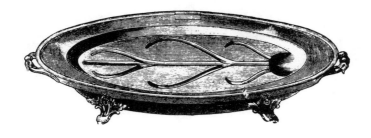

HEARTY CARIBOU STEW

Type B

4 slices bacon, diced
2 pounds caribou chunks
6 carrots
1 rib celery, sliced
2 medium onions,
  chopped

3 red potatoes, unpeeled,
  cut into four pieces
1 20 oz. can Italian
  tomatoes
1 teaspoon each oregano,
  basil, paprika

Brown bacon. Remove from kettle. Brown caribou in bacon fat. Push to side. Add carrots, celery, onions, and potatoes. Sauté in fat until vegetables are soft. Add tomatoes and seasonings. Cover and simmer one hour.

Serves 4–6

CARIBOU STEAKS

Types A-B

*1 to 2 pounds caribou
 steaks*
1 onion, sliced
1 cup tomato juice

¹/₂ cup flour
1 teaspoon paprika
¹/₂ cup oil

Trim steaks and cover with sliced onion. Cover with tomato juice and allow to stand at room temperature four to six hours. Remove from juice and pat dry. Dredge in flour. Sprinkle with paprika. Fry three to four minutes on each side until meat is golden. Drain on paper toweling. Place in a single layer in ovenproof pan. Bake at 300° for one hour. Serve with beef gravy, mushroom gravy, or the sour cream gravy recipe that follows.

Sour cream gravy:
1 pint sour cream
1 cup beef gravy
1 teaspoon paprika

Combine all ingredients and heat through.

Serves 4

CARIBOU STEW

Type B

2 pounds caribou stew
  meat, cubed and
  trimmed
¼ cup flour
¼ teaspoon paprika
4 oz. butter or margarine
  (one stick)
3 tablespoons olive oil

1 medium onion, chopped
1 clove garlic, minced
1 small zucchini squash,
  cut up
½ cup dry white
  Vermouth

    Shake the meat in flour mixed with paprika, to coat. Brown the meat in butter and oil in heavy pot. Add remaining ingredients, and simmer covered for two hours.

Serves 6

STEWED CARIBOU
Type B

2 pounds caribou stew
  meat
4 tablespoons margarine
  (one-half stick)
1/4 cup olive oil
1 pound mushrooms,
  cleaned and sliced

2 medium onions,
  chopped
1 cup beer
2 whole cloves

Brown the meat in the margarine and oil in a heavy pot. Add mushrooms and onion. Sauté until onion turns translucent. Add remaining ingredients and simmer, covered for two and one-half to three hours.

Note: Dark beer, ale or porter will produce a more savoury dish. Try bock beer, two tablespoons molasses, a few extra cloves and a pinch of cayenne for a subtley piquant "stewed" caribou.

Serves 6

SPANISH CARIBOU

1–1½ pound venison
   round
   steak
½ cup flour
salt and pepper to taste
½ teaspoon oregano
¼ cup bacon fat

1 can tomato soup
1 medium onion, sliced
1 green pepper, sliced into
   rings
1 can chopped chilies

Combine flour, salt, pepper and oregano. Dredge steak in seasoned flour. Melt bacon fat, and brown the steak. Cover with tomato soup, onions, green pepper. Cover pan, lower heat to slow simmer and cook one to one and a half hours. Using a fork, check for doneness: venison should flake apart. Top with the chopped chilies and run under the broiler for a few minutes.

Serve on a platter with some of the pan drippings ladled over the top.

Serves 4

MOOSE ROAST
Type B

4-pound moose roast
¹/₄ cup flour
1 teaspoon paprika
¹/₂ teaspoon oregano
2 tablespoons butter or
  margarine
2 tablespoons oil

1¹/₂ cups tomato juice
¹/₂ teaspoon garlic powder
  or 1 clove, crushed
4 carrots, sliced
3 onions, chopped
1 cup sliced celery

Mix flour, paprika, and oregano. Dredge meat in this mixture to coat all sides. Melt butter or margarine and oil in heavy kettle. Brown roast on all sides. Add tomato juice and the garlic. Simmer covered two to three hours. Add vegetables and cook one-half hour more, or until vegetables are tender. Serve with pot juices.

Serves 6–8

77

MOOSE SWISS STEAK
Type B

*2 pounds moose round
  steak*
¹/₂ cup hearty red wine
1 onion, sliced
¹/₂ cup flour
¹/₂ teaspoon paprika

2 tablespoons oil
1 cup diced celery
1 16 oz. can tomatoes
*1 tablespoon
  Worcestershire sauce*

Marinate steak in wine and sliced onion for at least four hours. Pat dry, and dredge in mixture of flour and paprika. In Dutch oven, brown in hot oil on both sides. Add the remaining ingredients, cover tightly, and cook in 250° oven for two hours. Thicken pan juices with a little cornstarch dissolved in cold water (two teaspoons cornstarch in one cup water). Serve with pan juice gravy.

Serves 4–6

MEXICAN MOOSE

2 chopped green peppers
1 cup chopped onions
3 tablespoons oil
2 cloves garlic, crushed
2 pounds ground moose

8 bay leaves
2 cups water
2 beef bouillon cubes
1 cup rice

Sauté peppers and onions in the oil until onions become translucent and peppers soften. Add garlic cloves and saute two to three minutes more. Remove garlic cloves and discard. Add ground moose and cook over medium heat, stirring until browned. Add bay leaves, cover and simmer just over half an hour.

Bring the water to a boil and add bouillon cubes. Stir to dissolve cubes. Add rice, lower heat and cover. Simmer ten to fifteen minutes or until all water is absorbed by the rice and each kernel is tender.

Remove bay leaves from the meat mixture and stir in rice. Simmer five minutes just to combine flavors.

Good with taco chips and an avocado salad.

Note: Never serve anything with whole bay leaves still in it. The stems of those dried leaves can puncture intestines and cause a great deal of distress. If you cannot remove the leaves before serving, break off the leaf away from the center vein and crumble just the leaf into the food, discarding stem.

Serves 4–6

MOOSE STEW

Type B

1 pound moose stew
  meat, trimmed and cut
  into cubes
3 tablespooons oil
4 medium potatoes, diced
3 ribs celery, diced
1 medium onion, chopped
6 medium carrots, sliced
1 16 oz. can stewed
  tomatoes

1 can tomato soup
1 soup can water
1 teaspoon basil
1 teaspoon paprika
1 teaspoon ground black
  pepper
1 garlic clove, crushed

Brown the meat cubes in the oil. Add remaining ingredients, and simmer covered on top of stove two hours, or cook in slow cooker on medium five to six hours.

This stew always reminds us of a huge "shadow" that followed us on a moonlight stroll through a Maine campground—a big moose leisurely strolling along behind us!

Serves 4

EASY ANTELOPE MULLIGAN

Type B

1^1/$_2$-pound antelope, cubed

1 medium onion, chopped

1 cup diced celery, including leaves

1 tablespoon margarine

^{1}/$_2$ cup uncooked rice

1 can golden mushroom soup

1 can cream of chicken soup

2 cups fresh mushrooms, washed and sliced

5 teaspoons soy sauce

1 cup peas

1 cup carrots

1 cup dry white Vermouth

Brown antelope, onion, and celery in butter. Mix together all remaining ingredients. Add all together to casserole, and bake uncovered at 300° two hours, or until meat is tender.

Serves 4

81

SNOWY DAY ANTELOPE STEW

¹/₄ cup flour
¹/₂ teaspoon salt
¹/₂ teaspoon cayenne pepper
¹/₂ teaspoon black pepper
2 pounds antelope, cut into 1" cubes
¹/₂ cup lard
3 medium onions, sliced and peeled
1 cup chopped celery
2 cloves garlic, crushed
1 can dark beer

1 tablespoon soy sauce
1 tablespoon steak sauce
1 tablespoon Worcestershire sauce
2 bay leaves
¹/₂ teaspoon dried thyme
3 tablespoons parsley
1 tablespoon honey
6 carrots, sliced thinly
6 medium potatoes, peeled and quartered
1 package frozen peas (10 oz)

Combine flour, salt and both peppers. Put in a plastic or paper bag and add 1 cup of antelope cubes at a time. Toss and pat to coat all pieces well. Repeat until all the meat is coated with the flour mixture. Set aside. Melt half the lard in a heavy skillet; sauté onion, celery and garlic. Remove vegetables from pan and add remaining lard. Sauté meat until browned on all sides. Return onion, celery and garlic to pan and add beer, soy sauce, steak sauce, Worcestershire sauce, bay leaves, thyme and parsley. Bring mixture to a boil. Add honey and stir to combine. Cover, reduce heat and simmer for two hours, or cook in crock pot on low setting for three to four hours. (If antelope is old or known to be tough, increase cooking time by one-half hour).

Cook carrots, potatoes, and peas in microwave or on top of stove. When meat is tender, add these cooked vegetables and heat through.

Serves 6–8

EASY ANTELOPE BURGUNDY

2 cans golden mushroom soup
1 package dry onion soup mix
1 cup Burgundy wine

3 to 4 pounds of antelope, cubed and trimmed

Mix the soups and wine to combine. Pour into slow cooker. Add the venison and stir. Cook on medium or low setting two and a half to three hours or until meat tests tender.

Note: This Antelope Burgundy is excellent served over rice. We prefer the long grain, brown variety. If you have a smoker, try smoking brown rice for this dish. It creates a stronger flavor statement that complements wild game.

Serves 6–8

ANTELOPE PAPRIKASH

2 pounds of venison
   round steak
$^1/_2$ cup flour
$^1/_4$ teaspoon basil
4 tablespoons paprika
$^1/_2$ cup butter
$^1/_4$ cup oil
2 medium onions, sliced

$^1/_2$ pound fresh mush-
   rooms, sliced
$^1/_2$ cup beef broth
salt and pepper to taste
2 tablespoons grated
   sharp cheese (romano)
$^1/_2$ cup sour cream

Trim steaks and leave whole. Combine flour, basil, one-quarter teaspoon of the paprika, then dredge steaks in the seasoned flour. Heat one-quarter cup of butter and the oil in a heavy skillet. Sauté onions and mushrooms until lightly browned. Remove from pan and add the remaining butter. Brown steaks on both sides. Stir in the remaining ingredients, cover skillet and cook over low heat thirty to forty minutes until meat is tender enough to come apart with a fork.

Serves 6

SAN ANTONIO CHILI

San Antonio natives swear this is the original American chili. They report it was developed in the San Antonio Jail to accommodate the cheap cuts of tough meat provided for the prisoners. Used with elk, this old recipe adapts very well, and is excellent for cuts of older game, such as moose, caribou, or antelope.

1/2 pound dry red beans
1 quart water
1/2 pound beef suet, ground
2 pounds elk or any red meat, cubed
3 garlic cloves, grated
1 1/2 tablespoons paprika
3 tablespoons chili powder

1 sweet red pepper
1/4 teaspoon cayenne pepper
1 tablespoon cumin seed
1/4 teaspoon salt
1 teaspoon black pepper
1 hot green or red pepper
1 can tomato paste
2 cups water

Wash red beans and pick through. Soak overnight in a quart of water. Fry suet in heavy kettle until browned. Add elk, and turn until browned. Pour water off red beans and add to meat. Transfer to a slow cooker. Add remaining ingredients and stir to combine. Cook on low setting six to seven hours or until meat falls apart and beans are tender. Add more water, if necessary, during cooking. Taste to adjust seasoning. Add more hot peppers if desired.

Serves 6–8 hearty appetites

LARGE GAME STOCK

6 pounds game bones, cut
  in pieces
2 teaspoons white vinegar
1 large onion, quartered
1 cup chopped celery

1 large bay leaf
4 large sprigs of fresh
  parsley
8 whole black peppercorns
2 teaspoons salt

Place bones in 2½ quarts of cold water and vinegar in large heavy pan. Simmer uncovered for 3½ hours. Avoid boiling. Add remaining ingredients and simmer 2 hours more. Strain and chill. Skim off fat. Use within 7 days or freeze in cup containers for future use.

Also see Down Home chapter for Homemade Condensed Beef Bouillon.

Fowl and Small Game

FOWL

*U*pland game birds are ground-dwelling. Their food consists mainly of insects, berries, and wild grains. They are excellent insect-controllers and are valued by farmers and country dwellers. Game birds can be found in every environment our country has to offer, from the marshes of the East and South to the prairies and deserts of the West and all the forests in between.

The fall hunting season for game birds is a blessing and a carefully designed plan for wildlife management in all sections of our country. As upland game birds are not migratory, many would die a slow and pitiful death of starvation were it not for the fall harvest.

The pheasant is a close relative to the domestic chicken and can be prepared very similarly. Ring-necked pheasants are natives of China that were brought to this country in 1881. They took to their new habitat with great adaptability and have thrived and multiplied ever since. They are especially numerous near the grain farms of the Great Plains. The ring-neck is perhaps the least wild-flavored of all the game birds; the flesh is mild and all white meat except for the legs.

The next important consideration is the age of the bird. In general, young birds will have short, round claws, while older birds will have developed longer, sharp claws. Young birds may be roasted or broiled and used in any fowl recipe with no special preparation necessary. Older birds, which you can expect to be tougher, should be braised or stewed. If you want to roast an older bird, use meat tenderizer to condition the meat. I suggest a flavored tenderizer, which will further minimize the wild taste. The older the bird, the longer it should stand with the tenderizer applied. Marinades of wine or citrus juice may also be used. A large bird, such as wild turkey, benefits from being tenderized in the refrigerator for 12 to 24 hours. Apply the tenderizer to the cavity, and rub under the skin of the breast.

Fish-eating fowl have rich dark meat that is almost always fishy tasting. Using only the breast meat, and marinating it at least 24 hours in vinegar and salt will minimize this problem. Use two cups of vinegar with four tablespoons of salt for the marinade. You may also use tenderizer on these birds after marinating them. Wash and dry the fowl before cooking. An apple quartered and placed in the cavity also absorbs some of the fishy taste.

To estimate the number of birds you will need for the number of people you are serving, follow these suggestions:

Game Bird Servings

One grouse will serve one to two people.
One partridge will serve one to two depending on size.
One pheasant will serve two to four depending on size.

Partridge, grouse, and pheasant are very similar in taste and texture. Recipes for pheasant may be used with partridge and grouse with equal success.

Game birds can be cut apart as you would a chicken. They tend to have thicker bones and skin than a domestic chicken, so use a sharp serrated knife or heavy poultry shears. Again, make sure you have removed the oil sacs on either side of the bird's spine before cooking.

Cut 1. Move leg back and forth to locate joint. Make cut as indicated through skin. Continue to move leg and cut leg from body and right through joint. After meat has been severed, bend leg away from you and down. This will cause the thigh joint to appear, making cutting through it easy.

Cut 2. Repeat with other leg.

Cut. 3. Cut down center of breast and spread bird apart. Rinse cavity and clean again, picking away organs or entrails and discarding.

Cut. 4. Using the bird's skeleton as a guide, cut breasts away from backbone.

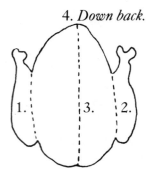

4. Down back.

From Field to Table

On an unseasonably hot day in Indian Summer, have you ever stopped in the supermarket, purchased a prime rib roast or a fresh turkey, put it in the trunk of your car and then gone to the movies? Unfortunately, a similar fate awaits something each autumn during the opening days of small game season. No wonder wild fare is not welcomed on some dinner tables. Neither would that hot prime rib or warm turkey make an appetizing entrée.

Successful cooking of game birds depends on several things—their condition, their age, and proper handling in the field. Care must be taken by the hunter to transport the game home in the best possible condition. Extra attention should be taken on a warm fall day because every hour in the field without refrigeration seriously affects the quality of the birds.

I even venture to suggest taking a cooler and a block of ice along if the weather is warm. Cleaned fowl can then be iced down as soon as someone can get back to the vehicle. Eviscerating immediately and taking time for thorough cleaning help to preserve all the delicate flavors.

Should you be caught far afield with no provisions to cool down game birds, a basket lined with leaves or moss and moistened is an effective way to protect them if the day is breezy. Under no circumstances should several birds be carried all day in a hunting-coat pouch near the body. Carrying game in this manner would render it inedible.

After the field-dressed bird has arrived in the kitchen, wash thoroughly in cold running water. Remove pin feathers and kidney and lung tissues on either side of the backbone. Cut off the oil sack at the back. Wash again, rinsing the inside of the bird well. Next, remove the feet and leg tendons, then make an incision down the center of the neck skin, so that the skin may be pulled away. Remove the neck by cutting off close to the body. The crop and windpipe may then be removed from this opening. Wash the bird one more time and refrigerate. Your game bird is now ready for the cook or the freezer. Be sure to date the packages and indicate whether the bird is young or mature.

ENGLISH BAKED PHEASANT

2 pheasants, skin on
1 pint ale or beer
1¹/₂ cups Italian seasoned
* bread crumbs*

2 eggs, beaten
1 teaspoon paprika

Cut unskinned pheasant into serving-sized pieces. Arrange in a deep dish or a sealable bag. Pour beer over fowl, and marinate two hours at room temperature. Remove from marinade and roll or shake in bread crumbs in a plastic bag or deep bowl. Dip in egg and again in bread crumbs. Generously sprinkle with paprika. Arrange on a cooky sheet or in a baking dish. Bake at 350° for one hour. Easy.

Serves 4

ELEGANT PHEASANT

Marinade
2/3 cup oil
1/4 cup white wine vinegar
2 tablespoons water
2 tablespoons finely grated
  onion
1 clove garlic, minced
1/2 teaspoon dried red bell
  pepper
1/2 teaspoon oregano
1/4 teaspoon basil
1/4 teaspoon sugar
1/4 teaspoon salt

4 to 6 cleaned and boned
  pheasant breasts
1 cup Italian seasoned
  bread crumbs
2 eggs, beaten with 2
  tablespoons water
4 oz. butter (one stick)
1/2 cup olive oil

Mix ingredients for marinade in a jar and shake to blend. Cover raw boned breasts with marinade. Marinate at least three days, turning twice each day. Remove breasts from marinade, but do not dry or drain. While they are still coated with marinade, dredge in bread crumbs. Dip in egg mixture, then in crumbs again. (Can be prepared to this point ahead of time and refrigerated until ready to cook.) Melt butter in electric frying pan. Add olive oil. Increase temperature to 350°. Sauté breasts until golden. Drain on paper towels. Can be held in oven on low setting, uncovered, for a half hour.

Note: Packaged Italian salad dressing mix prepared according to package instructions may be substituted for the marinade.

Serves 4

FRIED PHEASANT

Marinade
½ cup olive oil
¼ cup white wine vinegar
1 clove fresh garlic, crushed
1 teaspoon basil (fresh)
1 teaspoon fresh parsley
1 teaspoon fresh oregano (½ teaspoon dried)

1 cup seasoned crackermeal
¼ cup olive oil
½ stick margarine (do not use butter)
1 pheasant, cut into serving size pieces

Combine all ingredients for marinade. Arrange pheasant in a bowl or in a zip-lock type plastic bag and cover with marinade. Marinate overnight or for 2 days. Remove pheasant and dredge in crackermeal without draining. The marinade will make the crackermeal stick well. Pat the meal firmly into the fowl on all sides. Discard marinade or freeze for reuse.

Bring olive oil and margarine to 325° in an electric frying pan. This maintains an even heat, although a regular frying pan may be used. Fry until golden. Drain on paper towels. Serve hot.

Serves 4

PHEASANT FINGERS

Marinade
1/2 cup olive oil
1/4 cup white wine vinegar
1 clove garlic, crushed
1 teaspoon dried fennel, crushed
1 teaspoon fresh parsley
1 teaspoon fresh oregano (1/2 teaspoon dried)

1 cup seasoned crackermeal
1/4 cup olive oil
1/2 stick margarine (do not use butter)
2 whole breasts of pheasant

Combine all ingredients for marinade. Remove the breast meat from the bone and cut into finger size pieces. Place the meat in a bowl and marinate overnight. Remove the pheasant without draining and immediately dredge in crackermeal. Pat the meal firmly into the fowl on all sides. Discard marinade, or freeze for future use.

Bring olive oil and margarine to 325° in an electric frying pan. This maintains an even heat, although a regular pan may be used. Fry until golden. Drain on paper towels. Serve hot.

Serves 4 as an entree
6–8 as an appetizer

PEKING PHEASANT

4 to 6 pheasant breasts, cleaned

1 5 oz. bottle soy sauce

1 garlic clove, crushed

1 1/2 cups chopped Chinese cabbage

1 pound mushrooms, cleaned and sliced

1/2 cup slivered almonds

4 oz. butter or margarine (one stick)

In a large bowl or sealable bag, marinate the breasts in the soy sauce and garlic for four to six hours. Melt butter in large frying pan or wok. Sauté breasts three minutes per side, and remove. (Large breasts will take four to six minutes per side.) Add cabbage and sauté two minutes. Cover and steam 2 minutes. Add mushrooms and stir another two minutes. Return breasts to wok and reheat 2 to 3 minutes. Serve on heated platter with vegetables in the center and breasts around the edge. Garnish with almonds.

Note: This pheasant tastes best a little pink in the center. Do not overcook.

Serves 4

SUNCHOKE PHEASANT

6 pheasant breasts
1 pound Jerusalem
  artichokes, cut into
  half-inch slices
2 cups fresh or frozen
  orange juice

12 oz. frozen pearl
  onions
Paprika, salt, pepper,
  garlic powder to taste

Preheat oven to 325°. Place pheasant and vegetables in oven dish. Sprinkle on seasonings, pour juice over, and bake one hour. Easy.

Note: For more information on the Jerusalem artichoke or sunchoke, see page 151.

Serves 4

97

BARBECUED PHEASANT

1 16 oz. bottle of hot
   ketchup
1 8 oz. can crushed
   pineapple, undrained

2 pheasants, cleaned and
   cut into pieces

Blend first two ingredients in a blender or food processor. Skin the pheasant. Pour the sauce over the fowl, and allow it to marinate in the refrigerator three hours or more. Place pieces in baking dish and pour sauce over. Cover and bake at 300° for one and one-half hours or until birds test done.

This sort of preparation makes the basically dry pheasant very moist and tasty. This dish is a great way to have supper ready fast. Set the oven timer to turn the oven on after you leave the house, and let the birds marinate in the oven waiting to be cooked.

Barbecued pheasant can also be done in a microwave oven. Cover with plastic wrap and cook at low setting three minutes at a time, turning and resetting three times for a total of nine minutes. Check for doneness, and allow pheasant to rest several minutes before serving. Easy.

Serves 4

PHEASANT POT PIE

1 pheasant, cut up
2 tablespoons oil
2 chicken bouillon cubes
1 onion
1 teaspoon oregano

1 16 oz. package pot pie noodles
1 tablespoon butter

Brown pheasant pieces in oil in Dutch oven. Brown on all sides, until a rich brown crust forms on the bottom of pan. Add six cups of water, and bring to a boil. Add whole onion and bouillon cubes. Reduce heat and cook one hour, or until meat tests done. Discard onion. Remove fowl from broth, allow to cool and remove meat from bone. Add to the broth with oregano, salt and pepper to taste. Boil the noodles in the broth, then stir in the cooked pheasant. Allow butter to melt into broth.

Note: This makes a hearty winter meal. Serve with a big salad and a fruit dessert. Make Aunt Mag's noodles with the recipe from the Down Home section. They are worth the effort.

Serves 4

While visiting New Orleans, I was fortunate enough to meet the owner and driving force behind the New Orleans School of Cooking, Mr. Joseph Cahn. Mr. Cahn is a true disciple of Louisiana Cuisine and a native son his city can be proud of.

After attending his school, I couldn't wait to get home and improvise (as Joe encourages you to do) with pheasant and venison sausage and rabbit. Here are the resulting recipes—a taste of Louisiana à la wild game.

JOE CAHN'S JAMBALAYA

¹/₄ cup lard
*1 pheasant, cooked and
    meat removed*
*1¹/₂ pounds venison
    sausage, cut into bite
    sized pieces*
4 cups onion, diced
2 cups celery, diced
*2 cups green pepper,
    chopped*
1 garlic toe,* chopped

1 teaspoon paprika
*5 cups pheasant stock
    (page 80)*
3 heaping teaspoons salt
cayenne pepper to taste
4 cups long grain rice
1 cup green onion
*1 cup fresh parsley,
    chopped*

*In Creole cooking one segment of garlic is referred to as a "toe." Sometimes you will see this ingredient listed simply as "1 toe"!

100

Place pheasant in large pot and add seven cups of water. Bring to a boil and then reduce heat to simmer. Cook pheasant one-half hour, reserving liquid for stock and removing pheasant to cool. When fowl is cool enough to handle, remove meat from the bone and cut into bite size pieces.

Place lard in a heavy pot and heat until melted. Add the sausage and sauté 10 to 15 minutes until cooked and browned, stirring frequently. Remove from pot.

Add onions, celery, green pepper to the oil and saute until vegetables are tender (about 10 minutes). Remove from heat. Add sausage, pheasant and garlic, stirring well after each addition. Add the paprika at this time.

Pour the stock into the pot and return to heat. Bring to boil. Add salt, pepper and rice. Stir to combine and return to a boil. Cover and reduce heat to simmer. Cook for 30–35 minutes without peeking.

After 30 minutes, peek, stir and test rice for doneness. Add green onions and fresh parsley, stir and serve.

PHEASANT VEGETABLE SOUP

1 pheasant, cleaned
2 carrots, sliced
1 onion, chopped
2 ribs celery, with leaves,
    chopped
1 16 oz. can undrained
    tomatoes, quartered
1 cup fresh mushrooms
1 package frozen corn
1/2 package frozen peas

1 cup uncooked alphabet
    noodles
2 chicken bouillon cubes
1 teaspoon oregano
1 teaspoon paprika
1/2 teaspoon basil
1/2 teaspoon salt and
    pepper, or to taste
cooking liquid

In large pot, simmer the pheasant in water to cover (about two quarts). Simmer about one and one-half hours or until meat flakes off the bone. Remove fowl from pot, allow to cool, and cut into small pieces or shred. Add remaining ingredients to pot, return to boil. Continue to boil, stirring occasionally, until noodles are cooked through. Adjust seasoning. Add pheasant and let it heat through. Ladle into bowls.

Serves 4

CREAM OF PHEASANT SOUP

1 pheasant, cleaned and
  cut up
3 green onions, thinly
  sliced
¼ cup minced celery
  leaves
1 parsley sprig, minced

1 chicken bouillon cube
2 tablespoons rye or
  wheat flour
3 tablespoons butter
2 pints cream, or a 16
  oz. can of evaporated
  milk and a cup of milk

Brown pheasant pieces in oil in heavy pot, turning often. Add one cup of water, the onions, celery leaves, and parsley. Cover pot and bring to boil. Simmer one-half hour, or until meat is cooked. Remove meat from the pot, add bouillon cube, and boil stock to reduce liquid by half. Let pheasant cool before taking it off the bone and shredding. Melt butter in small pan. Add flour to make paste. Slowly stir in half of the milk or cream. Cook until cream sauce is smooth and thick. Add remaining milk or cream to the pheasant cooking pot. Slowly stir in cream sauce and blend. Add shredded pheasant. Garnish with paprika for color.

Serves 4

PHEASANT STOCK

If you use the recipes in this book calling for the breast meat of pheasant, the remaining pheasant pieces will make a good stock.

*1 pound of pheasant
    pieces
3 tablespoons oil*

*Water (about one quart)
Salt and pepper to taste*

Place a few pieces of pheasant at a time in a heavy pot and brown in the oil. Using medium heat, push aside and repeat until all the pieces have been browned and the pot has a golden crust. Scrape browned bits up and cover meat and bones with water. Simmer for two hours.

Remove meat and bones. Strain broth. Reserve for soups and sauces. This recipe may be doubled or even tripled. The broth freezes well.

Note: Meat scraps may be picked from the bones and included in soups.

STUFFED DUCK WITH SPICY FRUIT DRESSING

Stuffing
3 cups toasted bread cubes
rind of 1 orange, grated
1 teaspoon grated lemon
  rind
1/2 cup cubed orange
  sections
3 cups diced apple

3 tablespoons chopped
  onion
1 teaspoon salt
1/4 teaspoon ground cloves
1/2 teaspoon ground ginger
Pepper to taste

2 small ducks

Combine all stuffing ingredients, and fill body cavity of cleaned duck. Fill loosely and do not pack. This amount is enough for two small ducks or one four-pound duck. Roast in 350° oven for two hours, basting with orange juice. Increase heat to 425° for 20 minutes longer or until leg moves easily.

Note: After serving, remove the stuffing from the cavity and refrigerate any leftover meat. Never store any fowl with stuffing in the body cavity for this is conducive to bacteria growth.

Serves 2–4

BROILED BREAST OF DUCK

6 to 8 whole duck breasts,
 split, boned, and
 skinned
1 package Italian salad
 dressing mix, prepared
 according to directions
2 tablespoons
 Worcestershire sauce

1 clove garlic, crushed
$3/4$ teaspoon ground cloves
$1/4$ cup lemon juice
1 pound bacon

Soak duck breasts in salt water about three hours. Dry with paper towels, and place in a shallow pan.

Combine next five ingredients, and pour mixture over duck breasts. Place in refrigerator to marinate overnight. Remove duck from marinade, and wrap each breast in two or more slices of bacon. Place on broiling pan and broil about two inches from heat about seven minutes on each side.

Note: Serve with wild rice. This is a really special recipe.

Serves 4

FLORIDA GUMBO

2 large wild ducks,
  cleaned (2–3 pounds)
1 onion, chopped
4 ribs celery with leaves,
  chopped
1 15 oz. can chicken
  broth
1 pound hot smoked
  sausage, cut into one-
  inch pieces

$^1/_2$ cup oil
$^1/_2$ cup rye flour
1 green pepper, chopped
4 scallions, chopped
1 pound medium shrimp,
  cleaned and deveined

Place the ducks, onion, two of the celery ribs, and chicken broth in a Dutch oven. Add enough water to cover the ducks. Bring to a boil. Reduce heat and simmer about one hour. Remove ducks and allow to cool, reserving stock. Remove meat from bones and cut into bite-sized pieces.

Add sausage to stock. Pierce skin to release juices into stock. Simmer one-half hour. Heat oil in a heavy pot. Stir in rye flour. Heat 15 to 20 minutes, stirring constantly, until a nice roux is formed. Add remaining chopped celery, peppers and scallions and cook in roux ten minutes, stirring constantly. Gradually stir in reserved hot stock. Bring to a boil and simmer ten minutes uncovered. Add shrimp and simmer five minutes. Add duck, stir and heat through. Serve over rice. This is best made ahead of time and reheated.

Serves 8

MARTINI BAKED DUCK

Marinade
1 quart dry white
  Vermouth
2 cups water
1/2 cup safflower oil
1/4 cup melted butter
2 jiggers gin
1 onion reduced to juice
  in a food processor or
  blender
2 teaspoons ground
  pepper
1 dash red pepper sauce

2 large onions, quartered
8 bay leaves, cut in half
1 navel orange, chopped,
  with juice
1/2 cup chopped fresh
  parsley
8 wild ducks, cleaned,
  halved, and skinned

Combine first eight ingredients in a large Dutch oven. Remove half the mixture, and set aside. Heat the marinade to a simmer. Place duck halves, flesh-side down, into liquid in pan. Top each with a bay leaf, an onion section, chopped orange and parsley. Bake at 350° for three and one-half hours, basting occasionally. Remove from oven. Pour reserved Vermouth mixture over ducks, cover, and let stand in refrigerator for one to two hours, or overnight if desired. To serve, cover and bake at 350° for one-half hour or until heated through. Garnish with orange and parsley if desired.

Note: This is best prepared the day before serving, allowing flavors to blend and the cook to rest.

Serves 6–8

SMALL FOWL

S quab are young pigeons, but squab sounds so much more palatable than pigeons to most of us. They are considered a great delicacy and are usually expensive to buy. Squab should be served well-done. Allow one to two squab per serving, and expect it to be eaten with the fingers. The birds are too small to get all the meat off the tiny bones with a knife and fork.

ROAST STUFFED SQUAB

Stuffing
1/2 cup dry white wine
6 tablespoons butter
1 onion, minced
1 cup fine bread crumbs

1 cup brown crumbled
  sausage
1/4 cup chopped parsley

4 to 8 squab

Melt butter with white wine. Reserve half the mixture. In remaining butter and wine cook onion. Mix in bread crumbs, sausage, and parsley. Stuff each bird loosely with this mixture. Arrange in a baking pan and cover with foil. Roast at 325° for one-half hour. Begin to baste with the butter and wine mixture at quarter hour intervals until birds test done (about one and one-half hours in all).

Average appetites will require 2 squab per serving

SQUAB A LA CRAPAUDINE

1 to 2 squab per serving   Melted butter

Split each squab down the center of breast. Flatten with rolling pin. Broil under medium heat, turning several times and brushing well with melted butter. Cook until very tender and done, and browned on the outside. Season to taste.

110

BAKED SQUAB

Marinade for 4 squab
¹/₂ cut safflower oil
¹/₄ cup dry white wine

4 tablespoons butter (one-half stick)

Marinate squab in oil and wine. Brush with melted butter and bake at 325°, basting often with remaining butter. Allow two squab per serving. Increase marinade as necessary for larger numbers of birds.

Baked squab may be chilled and served cold as a picnic entrée.

OKLAHOMA QUAIL

4 cleaned quail

1 pound bacon

Wrap each bird in bacon, using about three or four slices per bird. Fasten with toothpicks or skewers, if necessary. Grill over a fire or charcoal, turning frequently. Remove skewers, and serve with brown rice.

Serves 4

Ruffed Grouse. This elusive bird has a large meaty breast and is very tender. The meat is predominantly white and the flavor mild.

SCOTT'S GROUSE

Clean and skin birds. Soak in salt water several hours. Rinse clean to remove salt and any blood. You will need the following for each bird:

3 slices bacon   *1 large apple*
2 large onions

For each bird, proceed as follows. Chop one onion coarsely and stuff into cavity of bird. Wrap in plastic wrap to seal out air, or place in plastic bag, squeezing out air. Refrigerate overnight. Remove onion and add to the cavity the second chopped onion and the apple, diced. Place the bacon slices over the breast and cover with foil, or put in baking pan with lid. Bake at 300° one hour, longer if you are roasting several birds. Test for doneness by moving leg bone. If leg moves freely, fowl is cooked.

1 bird per serving

WILD TURKEY PREPARATION

After the bird has been properly drawn and cleaned, and the breast skin detached from the breast, proceed as follows:

Generously sprinkle meat tenderizer on the breast meat under the skin. Rub into meat well with the hands. Sprinkle cavity with tenderizer, and refrigerate turkey several hours or overnight. To roast, remove bird from refrigerator at least an hour before stuffing. Allow to stand at room temperature. Fill the cavity of the neck end lightly. Fold skin over the back, and hold in place with a steel skewer. Now begin slowly and carefully packing the filling between the breast and the skin. Work patiently so as not to tear the breast skin. Place any remaining stuffing into the body cavity, filling lightly. Fasten this opening with skewers or sew up with heavy thread.

Roasting

Weigh the stuffed bird after it has been trussed, and allow 40 minutes per pound at 300°. Brush skin with melted shortening. Cover bird with a soft muslin cloth that has been dampened, then saturated with melted shortening. Place bird in oven, heavy part legs to the rear for even cooking.

ROAST WILD TURKEY

1 wild turkey
4 tablespoons butter or
    margarine (one-half
    stick)
1 large onion, diced
1 pound chorizo (Mexican
    sausage) or linguisa
    (Portuguese sausage)

1 16 oz. bread cubes or 6
    cups cubed bread
3 eggs

Clean bird. Soak in salted water one hour. Rinse and dry thoroughly. Melt butter in large pot. Sauté onion and celery until soft, stirring frequently. Remove from heat. Grate the sausage, or process with steel blade in the food processor. Add to celery and onion in the pot, along with the bread cubes and eggs. Mix well. Add a quarter cup of hot water to moisten. If a handful of stuffing will form a ball, it is moist enough. Add more water if necessary. Carefully loosen skin from breast by moving fingers slowly back and forth underneath skin until the entire breast skin is loose. (If skin splits, sew it back together.) Put filling between the skin and the breast, covering the entire breast. This should use all the filling as the skin stretches. This method of stuffing holds all the juices in the meat, making it moist and flavorful. Roast in a 300° oven for three to four hours, or 40 minutes per pound.

Note: A 20 to 22 pound domestic turkey is magnificent prepared in this manner, should your hunter not come through with a wild bird.

NEW ENGLAND WILD TURKEY

1 wild turkey
¹/₂ pound bacon, thickly
sliced

3 tablespoons softened
butter or margarine

Wash and dress turkey. Carefully loosen the skin from the breast. Place the thick slices of bacon on the breast, under the skin. Sew or skewer the skin and legs together, and brush the breast skin with the softened butter or margarine. Roast in a moderate oven at 350° until leg or wing moves freely, 40 minutes per pound.

Note: I prepare small domestic turkeys this way to cook them on a gas grill with a rotisserie. The bacon bastes the breast as the turkey cooks, imparting a subtle smoky flavor to the meat. Try this with chicken, too.

Serves 6–8

GLAZED WILD TURKEY

1 wild turkey
1 16 oz. can peaches in
  heavy syrup

1 cup pure maple syrup

Puree peaches with the maple syrup in a blender or food processor. Pour half of this mixture into the body cavity. Brush the surface of the bird with the glaze. Roast in a 250° oven two hours, basting every half hour during roasting. Increase heat during the last half hour to 350°. Roast 40 minutes per pound.

Serves 6–8

ROAST GOOSE

1 goose
2 cups sweet red
  Vermouth
1 onion

3 ribs celery, with leaves
2 tart apples, quartered
Flavored meat tenderizer
  (optional)

Place goose in deep container and pour Vermouth over bird. Turn frequently to coat entire body. Allow to stand overnight, turning at least four times. Cover marinating goose tightly with plastic wrap to prevent evaporation of wine. To roast, place all remaining ingredients in body cavity, put on rack in open pan, and roast slowly at 250°, allowing one-half hour per pound. Baste frequently with reserved marinade. This tastes remarkably like beef, and yields a very rich, all dark meat entrée.

Note: The feeding ground of all waterfowl determines the taste of the flesh. If a goose lived on fish and water animals, it will be strong and fishy. If it fed on corn and meal, it will be delicious and mild. Vary your marinating time to compensate for feeding areas. Allow one-half pound per person. If you fear the goose will be strong, fishy, or tough, sprinkle the body cavity generously with tenderizer and allow to stand another hour before roasting.

Serves 4

ROASTED BREAST OF OLD TOM TURKEY

1 whole breast wild
  turkey
2 cups sweet red
  Vermouth

1 large onion, sliced
Dash of paprika

Cut turkey breast in half and place in roasting pan or covered casserole dish skin-side down. Scatter the sliced onion on top of the breast, and cover with Vermouth. Marinate overnight. Bring turkey to room temperature and bake, covered, two hours at 250°. Remove lid of pan, and turn breasts skin-side up. Sprinkle with paprika, and roast uncovered until tender, at 350°. Depending on the size of the breasts, one-half to three-quarters of an hour more cooking time should be adequate.

Note: This is a good recipe for older birds. The slow simmer in Vermouth will make anything tender. Use the remaining turkey parts for soup.

Serves 4–6

STEWED SQUIRREL

2 squirrels, cleaned
$^1/_2$ teaspoon salt
$^1/_2$ teaspoon paprika
$^1/_4$ teaspoon pepper
Flour to coat

$^1/_4$ cup vegetable oil
1 small onion, sliced
1 sprig parsley, chopped
1 cup light cream

Cut squirrel into serving pieces, as for chicken. Sprinkle with salt, paprika, and pepper. Roll in flour to coat completely. Heat oil to 350° in skillet and brown squirrel well on all sides. Add onion, parsley, and cream. Cover pan and simmer one hour, or until done. (Meat will separate from bone and flake easily when cooked through.)

Serves 2

SQUIRREL CASSEROLE

3 or 4 squirrels
1¹/₂ cups chopped onion
1 cup mushrooms, sliced
6 cups cooked rice
1 teaspoon salt

1 clove garlic, crushed
¹/₂ teaspoon oregano
1 cup grated Muenster cheese

Cook game until tender in large pot with two cups water, covered, one hour. Reserve broth. Remove game and allow to cool before taking meat off the bones. Cut into bite-sized pieces. Add onion and mushrooms to meat. Put rice into casserole dish. Add meat mix on top, and sprinkle with seasonings. Thicken broth with 4 tablespoons flour and pour over all. Bake at 350° until heated through, about 45 minutes. Top with cheese, and run under broiler to brown.

Serves 4

SOUTHERN FRIED SQUIRREL

4 dressed squirrels
3 eggs
1 cup flour
¹/₂ teaspoon baking
*   powder*

¹/₂ teaspoon paprika
¹/₂ teaspoon oregano
1 cup oil

Cut squirrels into serving pieces. Beat eggs. Combine dry ingredients in a paper bag. Drop pieces of squirrel one at a time into the flour seasoning mixture. Dip in egg and repeat. Allow squirrel to stand for a few minutes to dry the coating. Heat oil at 375° until a bread cube browns. When oil is ready, fry squirrel until golden on all sides, about 12 to 15 minutes.

Serves 4

SQUIRREL À L'ORANGE

2 cleaned squirrels
1 cup evaporated milk
1 egg
1/2 cup orange juice

1/2 cup flour
1 to 2 ounces port wine
1/2 cup oil

Cut each squirrel into six pieces—four legs and two back pieces. Parboil in salted water for forty minutes. Drain squirrel pieces and pat dry. Beat egg and whisk into the milk. Slowly add one-quarter cup of the orange juice, reserving remainder. Dip squirrel into this batter, then roll it in the flour. Fry over medium heat in large skillet until golden. Drizzle remaining orange juice and the port wine over nearly cooked pieces.

When each piece can be easily pierced with a toothpick, they are done to perfection.

Note: L. James Bashline is an associate editor for *Field and Stream*, a columnist for *Pennsylvania Sportsman* and the outdoor columnist for the *Pittsburgh Post Gazette*. An outdoor enthusiast, author of several books and a fine hand in the kitchen, Jim claims this is his favorite squirrel recipe.

Serves 4

SOUPED-UP SQUIRRELS

3 squirrels
3 bay leaves
1 can mushroom soup

1 can evaporated milk
2 cups wild rice, cooked

Cut the squirrels into serving size pieces and simmer in water to cover with the bay leaves for three-quarters to one hour. Remove from pot and allow to cool. Remove meat from the bones and set aside. Combine mushroom soup with evaporated milk and simmer gently to heat through. Add the squirrel and stir to combine. Heat several minutes more, and serve over hot rice.

Note: From Paul Jukes, who says he uses this recipe for rabbits with equal success.

Serves 4

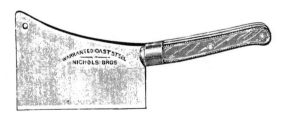

HARVEST SOUP

1 squirrel
1/2 pound hot venison
  sausage, chopped
1/2 pound smoked
  sausage, chopped
2 medium onions,
  chopped
4 medium potatoes, diced
1 package frozen mixed
  vegetables
2 16 oz. cans creamed
  corn

1 can evaporated milk
3 bay leaves
1 teaspoon seafood
  seasoning
1 teaspoon oregano
1 teaspoon black pepper
1/2 teaspoon salt
1/2 teaspoon paprika
1 medium-sized pumpkin
  to use as tureen

Clean, skin, and cut squirrel into pieces. Cover with two quarts of water and 1/4 cup salt. Allow to soak several hours. Drain, rinse, and pat dry. Cover with fresh water in pot and cook over medium heat one-half to three-quarters of an hour. Remove meat and allow to cool before picking meat from bones and cutting into small pieces. Add sausages and onion to a pot with two more quarts of water and bring to a boil. Lower heat and boil slowly for 15 minutes. Add potatoes and mixed vegetables, and boil five minutes longer. Add remaining ingredients, including squirrel meat. Lower heat to simmer, and cook one hour to allow flavors to mix. Stir frequently to prevent sticking.

For pumpkin tureen, heat oven to 300°. Wash pumpkin, and cut top off as for a jack-o-lantern. Remove seeds, put pumpkin on cooky sheet, and bake 20 to 30 minutes. You want the pumpkin heated, but not cooked through. It must stay firm enough to serve as a tureen.

Bring soup close to boiling, ladle into pumpkin, and serve. As you ladle individual bowls, scoop some softened, cooked pumpkin from the sides for garnish.

Note: This is our family's traditional Thanksgiving Eve supper. I serve it with a green leafy salad and a loaf of home-made egg bread. The pumpkin tureen is dramatic and the soup delicious. Try making the soup several days in advance, as it becomes even more flavorful as it ages. Of course it is just as good served from a real tureen.

Serves 6–8

RABBIT FRY

Marinade
2 cups dry white wine
1 cup vinegar
1 onion, minced
1 tablespoon minced
   parsley
6 whole black peppercorns
1 teaspoon salt

1 large (2 pounds)
   rabbit, or 2 small (1
   pound) rabbits, cut
   into serving pieces as
   for chicken
1 cup flour
1 teaspoon paprika

Combine first six ingredients. Pour marinade over meat and refrigerate for 24 hours. In a paper bag, combine the flour, paprika, and salt and pepper to taste. Shake rabbit pieces in flour and seasonings, then fry in hot oil until golden and done, about 20 minutes per side.

Serves 4

EASY FRIED RABBIT

2 average-sized rabbits
1 cup flour
1 teaspoon oregano
1/2 teaspoon salt

Dash of garlic powder to
taste
1/2 cup vegetable oil

Dress, wash, and cut up rabbits. Soak in salt water one-half hour. Rinse and cover with fresh water in a stew pot. Bring water to a boil, then lower heat and simmer uncovered until meat is tender, about 45 minutes. Remove pieces from liquid, and dredge, one at a time, in seasoned flour. Fry in oil until golden on all sides.

Serves 4

HASSENPFEFFER

1 rabbit, cut into serving
  size pieces
4 cups wine vinegar
1 tablespoon salt
1 tablespoon pickling
  spices
1 tablespoon peppercorns
2 bay leaves

1 cup chopped onions
2 tablespoons cooking oil
2 tablespoons flour
1 cup cold water
1 teaspoon cinnamon
1/2 teaspoon allspice

Place rabbit in a bowl or plastic bag and cover with vinegar. Add the salt, spices, peppercorns and one half cup of the onions. Marinate in the refrigerator for twenty-four hours. Drain, cover with boiling water and simmer about one and a half hours or until the rabbit is tender. Remove the meat from the bones and strain broth. Heat oil in a frying pan, blend in flour, stirring constantly to make a roux. Add the cup of water and whisk until smooth. Cook until thickened. Add the rabbit, 2 cups of the strained broth, cinnamon, allspice and remaining onion, and simmer for another hour. Serve over noodles.

Serves 2–4

GRANDMA'S HASENPFEFFER

1 rabbit, cleaned and cut
  into serving size pieces
2 cups water
2 cups white vine vinegar
1 onion, sliced
1 tablespoon peppercorns

1 teaspoon salt
2–3 whole cloves
2 bay leaves
4 tablespoons butter
1 cup sour cream

Place rabbit pieces into a bowl or plastic bag and cover with the water, vinegar, onion, peppercorns, salt, cloves and bay leaves. Allow to marinate in the refrigerator one to two days. Heat butter in heavy skillet. Brown the rabbit on all sides. Add one cup marinade liquid. Simmer covered one-half hour, or until meat is fork tender. Add sour cream and stir until heated through. Serve immediately.

Serves 2–4

HASSENPFEFFER

1 rabbit
Salt and pepper to taste
$^1/_2$ cup flour
$^1/_4$ cup vegetable oil
8 oz. hot ketchup
1 tablespoon cider
3 tablespoons cornstarch
dissolved in 1 cup
water

1 medium onion, chopped
2 bay leaves
$^1/_4$ teaspoon seafood
seasoning (Old Bay
preferred)

Cut rabbit into pieces, and salt and pepper each piece. Dredge in flour to coat. Fry in hot oil until just golden. Remove from fat and drain. Combine the vinegar and ketchup with the cornstarch mixture, and pour this into the skillet to combine with remaining oil. Stir over medium heat until gravy thickens, scraping bottom and sides of pan to incorporate browned bits into gravy. Add the onion, bay leaves, and seafood seasoning. Stir to combine. Return the fried rabbit to the gravy, cover, and simmer until tender.

Serves 4

BARBECUED RABBIT

1 2- to 2¹/₂-pound
   rabbit, or two small
   rabbits
1 cup flour
1 teaspoon salt
¹/₂ cup oil

Barbecue Sauce
1 16 oz. can whole berry
   cranberry sauce
1 bottle ketchup

Clean rabbit and cut into serving pieces. Dredge in seasoned flour, and brown in the hot oil. Drain. Combine the cranberry sauce and ketchup in a saucepan over medium-low heat. Stir to blend. Pour sauce over rabbit and bake at 350° 45 to 60 minutes, or until tender.

Note: This sauce is wonderful with squirrel, chicken, pork, or any fowl.

Serves 4

RABBIT PIE

1 2- to 2½-pound rabbit
1 cup flour
½ cup vegetable oil
2 to 3 medium potatoes, diced

2 onions, diced
2 carrots, sliced
2 tablespoons cornstarch
Biscuit dough

Cut rabbit into serving pieces. Soak in equal parts of vinegar and water for six hours. Drain and wipe dry. Dredge in flour until coated. Fry in hot oil just to brown. Add water to cover, and simmer slowly in covered pot for one hour. Add potatoes, onions, and carrots. Cook one-half hour longer, or until vegetables are done. Stir the cornstarch into ½ cup cold water, until combined. Add to liquid and stir until it is thickened. Turn the stew into a baking dish, and top with biscuit dough. Bake in a 400° oven 15 to 20 minutes, or until the dough is baked.

Serves 4

BISCUIT DOUGH

2 cups sifted flour
3 teaspoons baking
 powder
$\frac{1}{2}$ teaspoon salt

$\frac{1}{2}$ cup shortening
$\frac{2}{3}$ cup plus one
 tablespoon milk

Sift dry ingredients and cut in shortening until coarse crumbs form. Pour milk in center all at once and stir quickly until dough begins to hold together. Dough should be very soft. Knead 8 to 10 strokes, pat into a circle and cut rounds with a biscuit cutter or a glass. Place on top of stew with sides touching, covering top of casserole.

RABBIT BURGUNDY

1 1/2 cups hearty burgundy
3 green onions, sliced
3 cloves garlic, minced
1/2 teaspoon sweet basil

1/2 teaspoon thyme
5 peppercorns, crushed
2 rabbits, cut into serving
   size pieces
6 tablespoons oil

Combine the wine, onion, garlic, basil, thyme and peppercorns in a bowl or plastic bag. Add the rabbit and marinate several hours in the refrigerator, stirring several times.

Remove rabbit from marinade and pat dry. Sauté rabbit in oil until golden, but do not overcook. Drain rabbit and place in a baking dish. Pour marinade over and bake, covered, at 300° for one hour.

Serves 4–6

RABBIT STEW

1 small rabbit, cut into
  serving pieces
2 cups dried lima beans
  soaked overnight in $1^1/_2$
  quarts water
5 medium carrots, sliced
2 green peppers, chopped

1 medium onion, diced
1 clove garlic
2 bay leaves
2 teaspoons salt
$^1/_4$ teaspoon pepper
2 tablespoons butter

Place rabbit in boiling water with the drained beans and
$1^1/_4$ quarts of fresh water to cover. Add vegetables, garlic clove,
bay leaves, and seasonings. Simmer one hour, adding more
water if needed. Add butter for the last 15 minutes of cooking
time.

Serves 4

The secret to Joe's Gumbo is the roux. Use animal fat, keep the fat hot and the whisk moving, and it will come out perfect every time.

JOE CAHN'S NEW ORLEANS GUMBO

1 rabbit, cut into serving size pieces
1 cup lard
1¹/₂ pounds venison sausage, cut into pieces
1 cup flour
4 cups onions
2 cups celery
2 cups green pepper
1 garlic clove, chopped
8 cups stock (beef or venison)

Cayenne pepper to taste
Salt to taste (1–2 teaspoons)
1 cup fresh green onion
1 cup fresh parsley, chopped
Cooked rice (¹/₂–1 cup per person)
Filé to taste

Sauté the rabbit in lard, until golden on all sides. Remove from pot and allow to cool. Remove meat from bone. Sauté sausage in the lard. Remove.

For the roux, bring oil to just under spatter temperature, and being careful, using a long handled spoon add the flour all at once, stirring constantly. After flour is blended, use a whisk to incorporate flour into oil. Maintain heat. Stirring constantly, the roux will begin to get smooth and darken. Cook until a dark golden color is reached. The darker the roux, the stronger the gumbo.

Combine the onions, celery and pepper in a large bowl. Pour hot roux over vegetables in bowl and stir to combine. Add the chopped garlic to the vegetables and roux. (Never add garlic to hot ingredients.) Return this mixture to the pot and cook until a glaze forms on the vegetables and they are tender (about 10 minutes). Return rabbit and sausage to pot and cook on low heat. Gradually stir in stock and bring to boil. Reduce heat to simmer and cook for an hour. Season to taste with cayenne and salt. May be done up to this point ahead of time.

Ten minutes before serving, add green onions and parsley. Serve over cooked long grain rice. Filé may be placed on the table for individuals to add their own. One-quarter to one-half teaspoon per serving is recommended. (Never add filé during cooking.)

Note: Filé is the ground leaf of the sassafras plant. If added to soup or gumbo during cooking, it will thicken the broth beyond reason. It is available in most gourmet shops.

Serves 10–12

BRUNSWICK STEW NORMANDY WITH MILKWEED SHOOTS

1 squirrel
1 rabbit
1 pheasant
1 pound venison, cubed
2 medium onions,
  coarsely diced
1/2 cup green onions or
  scallions, sliced
4 stalks celery, diced, plus
  some of the young
  leaves, sliced
1 package frozen lima
  beans
1 cup fresh raw carrots,
  sliced

1 16 oz. can stewed to-
  matoes, with liquid
1 cup frozen peas
1 cup frozen corn
1/2 cup young, tender
  milkweed shoots
1/2 teaspoon oregano
1/2 teaspoon Bells Seasoning
1/2 teaspoon pepper
salt to taste
1/2 cup brandy

Gently poach squirrel, rabbit and pheasant using three cups of water in covered Dutch oven. Remove from broth, cool, and take meat from bones. Cut into bite size pieces. Brown venison quickly in dry pan at high heat for several minutes to sear in juices. Add strained broth from small game, along with the onions, celery, lima beans and carrots. Add squirrel, rabbit and pheasant pieces. Cook twenty minutes at slow simmer. Add tomatoes, peas, corn and milkweed shoots.

Simmer another thirty-five to forty minutes, stirring occasionally. Thicken if necessary with two tablespoons cornstarch and one-quarter cup cold water. Add brandy immediately before serving.

Serves 8–10

BRUNSWICK STEW

1 venison steak
1 pheasant, cut into pieces
1 squirrel, cut into pieces
4 potatoes, diced
4 ribs celery, chopped
3 carrots, sliced

1 onion, sliced
1/2 teaspoon oregano
Chopped parsley to taste
Salt and pepper to taste

Brown steak in oil in a heavy pot, and remove. Add game, one piece or two at a time, to brown. Remove pieces when browned, and repeat until all meat and fowl have been browned. Do not crowd, as the meat will steam instead of brown. Add one quart of water to the pot and stir to incorporate pan juices and browned film on pan bottom. Bring water to a boil, and add all the meat pieces. Reduce heat and simmer one hour, or until meat tests done. Remove meat from pot. Cool. Take meat off bones and cut into bite-sized pieces. Add vegetables and seasonings to the pot with the broth. Simmer until cooked, about 20 minutes. Thicken if desired with flour or cornstarch paste. Add meat and reheat. Season to taste.

Serves 6–8

Natural Foods

WILD GREENS AND VEGETABLES

 he American Indian taught the first settlers much about how to survive on food found in field and forest. Cooking in many areas of the country comes from these humble beginnings. Indian women knew many ways with wild food that are interesting to try today.

The Indians of Cape Cod ate what they called girasol. Girasol is what we know as Jerusalem artichoke. The cigagawunj, or wild garlic, saved many from starvation. It was prolific in an area the settlers later named for it—Chicago.

The Indian woman served pigweed, sorrel, evening primrose, dock, and hedge mustard in salad. She used the tender young shoots of the cattail as a vegetable very similar to the way we use asparagus. Rocky Mountain beeweed was the Indian's spinach. Venison was often cooked with dandelion and seasoned with maple sugar.

Indian women used flowers to add zest to their diet as well as nutrients. They added milkweed blossoms and buds to meat soups for flavor and thickening. They fried the delicate redbud and boiled the buds of at least 15 other flowers, including marigold, clover, and pokewood to make jams and relishes as well. The Indian ate over 50 varieties of greens. Marion and G. L. Wittrock, in a survey for the New York Botanical Garden, state that the American Indian ate the berries and fruits of nearly 300 different plants. Little wonder they had so much to teach the trapper and explorer of our new land.

The sweet tooth was satisfied by maple sugar and cattail sap candy. Milkweed blossoms were used to sweeten, as was the morning dew that clung to the blossoms. Today we can try sweetening wild strawberries by shaking the early morning dew from milkweed blossoms over sun-ripened berries. Next time you gather blueberries, line a basket with fresh sweet fern to preserve the wild woods fragrance on the journey home, as our Indian teachers did.

Acorn meal was made by soaking acorns overnight until the shell split open. The kernels were picked out and spread in baskets to dry, then ground into flour. Indians were inventive and persistent, developing a rich and varied diet seemingly by instinct.

Could the average American today exist for a week without his customary food?

Certainly survival in the wild is not likely to be required of the average American. Taking a cue from our country's original people, however, you can use some of their ancient wild accompaniments to enhance your diet, particularly with wild game recipes.

The recipes that follow reward you with more than taste and nutrition: the exercise and tranquility one experiences while gathering these ingredients. Getting in touch with the natural world and enjoying the out-of-doors is an excellent step toward a healthier body. Meals prepared with wild foods are a creative challenge, more than just a simple solution to hunger. A natural meal prepared with wild game and wild side dishes requires a commitment of love and patience that nourishes the soul as well as the body.

Spring fields yield tender young dandelion leaves, delicate fiddlehead ferns and mild lamb's tongue, while streams offer peppery watercress. The warmth of the sun soon ripens the beautiful wild strawberry just as it did for the Indians

143

long ago. Summer yields blueberries, raspberries, blackberries, and grapes as well as edible roots and flowers.

Edible Flowers

Violets, honeysuckle, and wild roses are available in abundance, and add a sweet flavor to cold soups, punches or salads. Marigolds and nasturtiums impart a peppery taste that goes well with cheese, egg dishes and batters. Pansies, peonies, tulips, lilies, and chrysanthemums are also edible.

Use only fresh flowers, or store in the refrigerator if you must hold them for any period of time.

Try some of these recipes, and I hope you will be pleasantly surprised. If you are unfamiliar with wild plants, and this section interests you, I suggest you read some books by Euell Gibbons or Bradford Angier for more detailed information and identification techniques.

FERNS

The coiled fronds of the brake fern, or pasture brake fern (Pteridium aquilinum) and the ostrich fern have been used by Native Americans for centuries in salads and soups. Hunters would do well to consume raw fern in quantity when stalking deer with a bow and arrow because the deer feed upon these ferns. If the hunter is ingesting the same food as the animal he is stalking, his breath will not betray him. Eating raw brake fern fiddleheads may enable a hunter to approach to within twenty to thirty feet of a deer without his scent giving him away. This Indian trick really works.

Fiddleheads are the uncurled fronds of several species of edible ferns. Most fiddleheads are consumable, although the species we mention have the most pleasing flavor. (For more specific information and field identification, consult *Edible Wild Plants of Eastern North America,* by Merritt Lyndon Fernald and Alfred Charles Kinsey, or *Free for the Eating* by Bradford Angier.)

Fiddleheads are very versatile. They may be added to any green vegetable dish, or served steamed and buttered by themselves. They are good stir fried, and can be added to salads and soups.

The fiddleheads should be blanched in boiling water for a few minutes before steaming. They have a slight almond taste that gives salads and soups a different, pleasant taste similar to okra.

Mature fern fronds are tough, taste badly, and some may be poisonous, including the pasture brake fern. They are so tough and distasteful, however, that it is not likely anyone would choose to eat them.

The tender fiddleheads are three-forked and are best eaten when they are five to eight inches high while still rusty with a fuzzy coating. Break them off as low on the plant as they will snap, and rub the fuzz off between the fingers. They are now ready for eating raw or ready for cooking.

FIDDLEHEAD FERN SALAD

2 cups fiddleheads
½ head iceberg lettuce
1 8 oz. can water
   chestnuts

Oil and vinegar

Steam the blanched fiddleheads until just cooked, two to three minutes. Tear lettuce into bite-sized pieces. Slice water chestnuts. Toss together, and add oil and vinegar to taste.

Serves 4

FIDDLEHEAD SOUP

1 quart broth—pheasant,
   chicken, or quail
2 chicken bouillon cubes
1 cup blanched
   fiddleheads

1 cup cooked shredded
   fowl meat of your
   choice

Bring broth to a boil and add bouillon cubes. Reduce heat and add fiddleheads. Simmer 3 minutes. Add meat. Heat through and serve. This makes an unusual and elegant first course.

Serves 4

DANDELION SPINACH SALAD

¹/₂ bowl dandelion leaves
¹/₂ bowl spinach leaves,
broken
1 16 oz. can fried onion
rings

Prepared Italian
dressing, or oil and
vinegar

Toss greens to mix. Chill. To serve, add dressing and garnish salad with onion rings.

Serves 4

WILTED DANDELION

1 medium-sized bowl
dandelion leaves,
cleaned

6 slices bacon
¹/₃ cup white wine vinegar

Use only young tender leaves that have been thoroughly cleaned. Break into bite-sized pieces. Dice the bacon and fry until crisp. Remove bacon from pan and add vinegar. Bring to boil, scraping the pan to include any bacon bits. Add the greens, tossing in hot liquid until wilted and heated through. Season to taste with salt and pepper, garnish with bacon, and serve immediately.

Serves 4

PENNSYLVANIA DUTCH DANDELIONS

1 bowl dandelion leaves, cleaned
6 slices bacon, diced
3 green onions or wild chives, chopped

¹/₃ cup white wine vinegar
2 teaspoons cornstarch

Sauté bacon until crisp. Remove bacon with a slotted spoon and drain. Add vinegar to pan and stir. Reheat until boiling, stirring constantly. Make a paste with cornstarch and ¹/₂ cup of water. Slowly stir into vinegar. Simmer to make hot gravy. Pour over greens in bowl and garnish with green onions and bacon. Serve immediately.

Serves 4

CREAMED DANDELION

2 pounds dandelion
  greens
5 slices bacon
½ onion, minced
1 egg, beaten

¼ cup vinegar
2 tablespoons water
2 tablespoons sugar
1½ tablespoons flour

Wash dandelion greens thoroughly under running water. Cook in covered kettle with plenty of salt until tender. Remove and drain. Chop bacon and brown in same pot. Add onion and stir until golden. Add egg, vinegar, water, sugar, and flour to pot. Stir to combine and heat slowly, stirring until thickened. Pour hot dressing over greens and mix well. Garnish with sliced hard-cooked eggs, if desired.

Serves 4

DANDELION CASSEROLE

2 pounds dandelion
  greens, chopped
1/2 cup flour
4 tablespoons butter (one-
  half stick), melted
1 cup cream

1/2 teaspoon salt
Dash pepper
1/2 cup grated Swiss cheese
1/2 cup cracker crumbs

Arrange greens in layers in greased baking dish, sprinkling with flour between layers. Combine butter, cream, salt, and pepper. Pour over greens. Combine cheese and crumbs. Top greens with cheese mix, and bake at 350° for 35 minutes.

Serves 6

JERUSALEM ARTICHOKES

*T*he Indians of Cape Cod grew a root of a variety of sunflower, a tuber they called *girasol*. The girasol patch was cultivated only by men, although women tended the rest of the garden crops. Explorers took a sample back to Spain, and in a few years the girasol was popular all over Europe as the Jerusalem artichoke.

Today you may see Jerusalem artichokes marketed as sunchokes. Sunchokes are a good source of iron, while low in fat, sodium, and calories. They have a crisp texture and a pleasing nutty flavor. Wash and scrub them well, and for maximum nutrition do not peel. Sunchokes may be eaten raw in salads or sliced and used with a dip. They are excellent sautéed, steamed, pickled, or baked. They can be added to casseroles for flavor and nutrition.

Cooking Method Number One

Scrub 1 pound sunchokes and cut into uniform pieces. Boil or steam until tender. Toss with butter and lemon juice, and garnish with parsley.

Cooking Method Number Two

Scrub artichokes and cut into uniform pieces. Drop into hot fat and fry until golden brown. Serve with ketchup.

Cooking Method Number Three

Scrub 1 pound artichokes. Grate on coarse grater. Add one-half onion, grated. Sauté in butter until onion is golden and chokes are crisp-tender. Sprinkle with paprika for color.

Serving Suggestion: Use this vegetable raw in salads. Grate or slice.

SUNCHOKE PICKLES

2 quarts cubed sunchokes
1 quart white vinegar
1¹/₄ cups sugar
1 clove garlic

1¹/₂ teaspoons turmeric
2 tablespoons mixed
* pickling spices*

Make a brine using one cup of salt to a gallon of water. Stir and let salt dissolve. Put sunchokes into a large enameled or stainless steel pot, and pour in brine to cover. Let stand overnight. Rinse, drain, and pack vegetable into clean jars. Combine remaining ingredients and simmer for 15 minutes, then boil for about ten minutes. Pour this mixture over sunchokes in jars until jar overflows. Screw on lid. Cool and refrigerate for 24 hours. Pickles will be sunny yellow on the outside and white on the inside.

SUNNY SUNCHOKE (JERUSALEM ARTICHOKE) SIDE DISH

*1 cup scrubbed and sliced
    sunchokes
1 teaspoon lemon juice
¹/₄ cup chopped onion
3 eggs
¹/₂ cup cream*

*¹/₂ teaspoon salt
¹/₂ teaspoon pepper
¹/₂ pound Swiss cheese,
    grated*

Put sliced sunchokes in water to cover. Add lemon juice, and boil covered about ten minutes or until chokes are tender when pierced with a fork. Drain, and place sunchokes in blender or processor with onion, eggs, cream, salt, and pepper. Blend until smooth. Stir in grated Swiss cheese. Pour mixture into small well-greased casserole. Bake 45 minutes at 350° uncovered or until custard is set. Cool ten minutes before serving.

Serves 4

CREAMED SUNCHOKES

1 pound sunchokes
5 tablespoons butter
5 tablespoons flour
1¹/₂ cups evaporated milk
¹/₄ teaspoon white pepper

¹/₄ teaspoon nutmeg
3 green onions, sliced
¹/₄ cup heavy cream
1 cup grated Gruyere cheese
1 egg yolk

Clean, peel and slice the sunchokes. Cover with water and simmer until tender. Drain and set aside. Melt four tablespoons of the butter in a saucepan and add the flour slowly, whisking to combine. Add the milk, pepper and nutmeg, stirring until the white sauce is smooth and thick. Heat the remaining tablespoon of butter and sauté the onions just until they are coated with butter. Add the cream, stir through, then add the cooked sunchokes, cream sauce and three-quarters cup of the cheese. Cook over low heat, stirring constantly until cheese melts. Beat the egg yolk until light in color, stir in and simmer ten minutes more. Pour into a baking dish, sprinkle with the remaining cheese and run under the broiler until bubbling and glazed. Serve immediately.

Serves 4–6

WILD LEEK SOUP

3 tablespoons butter
2 tablespoons olive oil
2 pounds wild leeks,
   sliced

6 cups rich beef broth
1 teaspoon paprika
Parmesan cheese for
   garnish

Heat butter and olive oil together in heavy pot. Add leeks and cook over medium heat until leeks are golden. Stir in broth, paprika, and salt and pepper to taste. Cover and simmer one hour. Serve garnished with grated Parmesan cheese

Serves 4

LEEK VICHYSSOISE

3 cups thinly sliced leeks
2 tablespoons butter
3 cups mashed potatoes

2 cups half-and-half
2 cups milk
Parsley to garnish

Sauté the leeks in butter until golden. Add mashed potatoes, and stir while adding the cream and milk. Add salt and pepper to taste, and heat through. Add more milk if soup is too thick. Garnish each bowl with chopped parsley.

Serves 4

WILD RICE

Wild rice is not a true rice as we know it, but a wild grain that grows in marshy areas. Because it is inaccessible and difficult to harvest, it is very expensive. Should you be fortunate enough to have a source of wild rice available to you, it is well worth the effort and time to gather enough for a meal. It is also worth the expense to buy wild rice occasionally. One cup of wild rice will feed four people.

Wild rice was a staple of Ojibway Indian diet. They called it the "good berry." During the milk stage of the rice, they set up camp and staked out preserves to delineate individual harvest rights. The grain was harvested by men in canoes, roasted, and then threshed using a bucket sunk into a hole in the ground. An Indian wearing new moccasins would then balance himself with two poles as he trampled the grain in the bucket. The chaff was blown away by shaking shallow trays of the grain in a gentle breeze.

Wild rice was cooked in venison broth and seasoned with maple sugar.

WILD RICE WITH MUSHROOMS

1 cup wild rice
4 cups water, boiling
¹/₂ pound mushrooms,
   sautéed

Butter to taste

Wash rice and slowly add it to the boiling water, not allowing the boil to be interrupted. After all the rice has been added and the boil is maintained, reduce heat to simmer, cover, and allow to cook at lowest setting for 35–40 minutes or until the water is absorbed and the rice tests done. Drain and mix with mushrooms and butter to serve.

Serves 4

FRIED WILD RICE

1 cup wild rice
4 cups water
¹/₄ cup vegetable oil

1 egg, beaten
2 tablespoons soy sauce

Wash rice and slowly add to boiling water. Stir and resume boil. Immediately reduce heat and simmer 35–40 minutes or until tender and water is absorbed. Drain.

Heat oil in skillet. Add rice and stir. Pour soy sauce over and continue stirring until rice is golden. Slowly drizzle beaten egg over rice and stir quickly to distribute throughout rice. Serve immediately.

Serves 4

SORREL

S orrel, or sour grass, has been consumed by man since 3000 B.C. Sorrel tastes slightly sour as its name implies, reminding one of spinach with lemon. Sorrel is widely used in Russia and in Europe where the Troisgros brothers in Rouen, France, were awarded a third Michelin star for their celebrated Poached Salmon in Sorrel Sauce. The French also enjoy it in their classic soup, *Potage Germiny*.

Sorrel grows in great profusion all over our continent. *Rumex acetosella*, often referred to as Sheep Sorrel, Field Sorrel, or Sour Grass, is easy to identify, even for the uninitiated. It grows about eight to twelve inches high and has pale green leaves shaped like arrowheads. This plant grows from early spring through summer, and some areas even produce a fall crop. Look for sorrel in fields, along roadsides, in gardens, and lawns. The leaves are small, between one and four inches long, and have a soft texture.

For further information consult a field guide to edible plants. To prepare, remove the stems and wash the leaves under cold running water. Cook as you would spinach, with just the water that clings to the leaves. A pound of sorrel will reduce to one-half to three-quarter cup of purée. The purée can be frozen for up to three months.

Add sorrel to soups and egg and fish recipes for a variation that is refreshing. Add one cup of julienned sorrel leaves to cream soups. Try adding sorrel as a garnish to hot soups, letting the leaves "melt" into the soup one or two minutes before serving.

POACHED FLOUNDER IN SORREL SAUCE

4 cups water
1/4 cup dry white wine
2 green onions, chopped
1 carrot, julienned
1 celery rib, with leaves, diced
1 bay leaf
1 large parsley sprig

8 black peppercorns
2 1/2 to 3 pounds flounder filets
Sorrel Sauce (recipe follows)
Chopped fresh chives and sorrel leaves for garnish

Preheat oven to 325°, and combine water and wine with vegetables and seasoning. Bring to a boil. Reduce heat and simmer 20 minutes.

Clean and dry filets. Season with salt and pepper. Place in baking dish in single layer. Pour in liquid and vegetable mixture. Cover with foil and perforate. Bake one-half hour, or until fish still feels firm but flakes. Lift fish from liquid, place on serving platter, and allow to cool. Cover cooled fish with chilled sorrel sauce, and keep refrigerated until serving. Garnish with chives and sorrel leaves.

Serves 4 to 6

SORREL SAUCE

2 cups washed sorrel
  leaves
1 cup washed spinach
  leaves
1 cup boiling salted water
2 eggs
2 teaspoons Dijon
  mustard

2 teaspoons dry white
  wine
1 cup peanut oil
3 tablespoons minced
  green onions

Add spinach and sorrel leaves to water and cook two to three minutes. Drain thoroughly, pressing out all moisture. Chop finely and reserve.

In blender or food processor combine eggs, mustard, and wine. Blend until smooth and then add oil, a small amount at a time, until mixture is thick and smooth. Add spinach and sorrel mixed with onions, and blend again. Season to taste with salt and pepper. Chill. Can be prepared one or two days ahead of time.

Makes enough sauce to top fish filets for 4–6

PINWHEELS

*1 loaf unsliced white
  sandwich bread*
1 cup watercress, chopped

*1 8 oz. package cream
  cheese, softened*
Pepper to taste

Cut bread lengthwise in slices one-half inch thick. Remove crusts. Combine watercress, cream cheese, and pepper. Spread a quarter cup of filling on each slice. Roll up, starting from the narrow end. Wrap each slice in plastic wrap, pulling tightly. Chill. Slice one-half inch thick to serve.

Makes two dozen

WATERCRESS CHEESE BALL

*2 ribs celery, finely
  chopped*
1 teaspoon olive oil
1 teaspoon vinegar
2 tablespoons mayonnaise

Pinch of saffron
*1 8 oz. package cream
  cheese, softened*
*1 bunch watercress,
  cleaned and chopped*

Mix first six ingredients in blender or food processor until blended. Form into a ball. Roll in chopped watercress to cover. Chill, and serve with crackers.

Serves 6–8 as one of several appetizers offered

WATERCRESS DIP

1 4 oz. package cream
   cheese, softened
¼ cup chopped watercress
2 tablespoons mayonnaise

2 teaspoons minced leek
1 teaspoon grated onion
Dash Worcestershire sauce

Combine all ingredients, and serve with fresh vegetables or on crackers.

Serves 2 to 4, as one of several appetizers offered

LEBANON WATERCRESS ROLLS

1 8 oz. package cream
   cheese, softened
1 bunch watercress,
   chopped (1–1½ cups)

1 pound Lebanon
   bologna, sliced slightly
   thicker than for
   sandwiches

Blend cream cheese with chopped watercress. Spread on each slice of meat. Roll up. Slice into pinwheels. Serve chilled.

Makes three dozen

WATERCRESS SALAD

1 large bunch watercress
  or enough to equal the
  size of a head of lettuce
1/2 cup bean sprouts

1/4 cup sliced water
  chestnuts
3 green onions, chopped
1 hard-cooked egg, sliced

Clean watercress, stem, and toss with remaining ingredients, except egg. Garnish with sliced egg, and serve with oil and vinegar dressing.

Serves 4

WATERCRESS SOUP

2 cups water
1 teaspoon seafood
  seasoning
1/2 large leek, diced
1/2 cup bamboo shoots
1/4 cup butter

2 cups chicken stock
1 cup chopped, cleaned
  watercress
1 egg, beaten

Simmer first five ingredients 15 minutes. Add stock and heat through. Add watercress, heat to boiling. Drizzle in egg and heat to serving temperature, stirring constantly.

Serves 6

CREAM OF WATERCRESS SOUP

1 bunch watercress, cleaned

4 tablespoons butter (one-half stick)

1 cup chopped leek

5 medium potatoes, peeled and diced

2 cups chicken stock

2 cups water

1 pint heavy cream

Reserve some perfect watercress leaves for garnish. Chop remaining watercress or process with steel blade in a food processor. Heat butter in a soup kettle over medium heat. Sauté until heated through. Add the watercress and potatoes, and cook until translucent. Add chicken stock and water, and bring to a boil. Cook five minutes. Blend or process until smooth. Return to heat and bring to serving temperature after cream has been added. Garnish with reserved leaves. Serve immediately.

Serves 6

SPINACH AND VIOLET SALAD

4 cups small spinach
  leaves, washed well
  and dried
2 pink grapefruit, peel
  and pith cut away
2 small fennel bulbs,
  sliced thin crosswise
4 teaspoons red wine vin-
  egar

1 tablespoon fresh pink
  grapefruit juice
$1/4$ teaspoon Dijon-style
  mustard
2 tablespoons olive oil
20 fresh purple violets

Divide the spinach between four chilled salad plates. Slice the grapefruit into thin slices and arrange on top of spinach. Place fennel on one side of the plate.

In a small bowl, whisk together the vinegar, juice, mustard and pepper to taste. Add the oil in a stream, whisking, until the dressing is emulsified. Pour over salad, arrange violets decoratively on top and serve immediately.

Serves 4

JO NATALE'S FRIED FLOWERS

2 eggs
¹/₂ cup milk
1 cup flour
1 teaspoon baking powder
¹/₄ teaspoon salt

¹/₂ teaspoon vanilla
1 teaspoon corn oil
2 dozen zucchini or
  pumpkin flowers
corn oil for frying

Pick flowers in the morning when they are open. Remove the stamen and the pistil from each. Rinse and refrigerate until ready to use.

Beat the eggs and stir in the milk. Sift together the flour, baking powder and salt. Beat in the oil and combine well.

Preheat oil to 350°. Gently dip flowers in batter and drop into oil, several at a time for a minute, or just until batter is golden. Drain and serve immediately.

Serves 4

MARIGOLD AND BROCCOLI CAVATELLI

4 garlic cloves, chopped
1 ounce olive oil
1 head broccoli, chopped
2 cups chicken broth
1 pound homemade or
  frozen cavatelli

4 tablespoons butter
3 fresh marigolds, petals
  removed
4 whole marigolds for
  garnish
1/2 cup grated Parmesan
  cheese

In a wok or frying pan, sauté chopped garlic in oil. Before it browns, add broccoli and stir-fry quickly. Add broth to cover broccoli and cook on a low flame until tender. Cook cavatelli to desired doneness. Place butter on cavatelli and toss to coat. Pour broccoli over cavatelli and top with marigold petals. Garnish with whole marigolds. Pass the cheese to be added at table.

Serves 4

MARIGOLD CHEESE SPREAD

1 (8 oz.) block cream
  cheese

3 to 4 fresh marigold
  flowers

Allow cream cheese to come to room temperature. Wash and shred marigold petals. Blend the petals into the cheese with a fork. Garnish with a whole flower if desired. Refrigerate until firm. Serve with crackers or sliced rounds of toasted French bread.

GORGONZOLA NASTURTIUM SALAD

1 head Boston lettuce
2 navel oranges
¼ cup gorgonzola, crum-
  bled

6 nasturtium petals, torn
  into pieces
4 whole nasturtiums

Divide cleaned and torn lettuce between four chilled salad plates. Cut the peel from the oranges and slice thinly. Place two orange slices on each plate; sprinkle with gorgonzola and nasturtium petals. Garnish with whole flowers. Serve with oil and vinegar dressing.

Serves 4

LASAGNE ROLLS WITH PICKLED NASTURTIUM BUDS

½ *pound mushrooms, sliced*
1 *cup ricotta cheese*
1 *cup pickled nasturtium buds*
1 *pound lasagna noodles, boiled*

1 *can of pitted, small, black olives, sliced*
2 *cups marinara sauce*
¼ *cup parmesan cheese, grated*

Microwave or sauté mushrooms until half done, and drain well. Mix together ½ of the nasturtium buds, mushrooms and ricotta until blended. Cut each noodle in half. Place a dollop of cheese mixture on one end of a lasagne noodle. Top with black olive slices and roll up jelly roll style, several turns. Place rolls in a baking dish, seam side down. Top with your favorite marinara sauce. Bake thirty-five to forty minutes at 375° or until heated through. Sprinkle on cheese and serve.

Serves 4

PICKLED NASTURTIUM BUDS

1 cup unopened nasturtium buds
¹/₄ teaspoon fennel seeds
¹/₄ teaspoon cumin seeds

3 tablespoons lemon juice
¹/₄ cup water
1 teaspoon honey

Scald a one-cup jelly jar and a canning lid band. Pack buds, cumin and fennel seeds in the jar.

Bring vinegar, lemon juice, water and honey to a boil. Stand the jar in hot water. Pour the boiling liquid over buds leaving a half-inch headspace at top of jar. Screw on canning lid, cool jar on a wire rack, and store in refrigerator for at least one week before using to allow flavors to blend. Use within two months.

Note: from *Rodale's Basic Natural Foods Cookbook*, Rodale Press, Emmaus, PA, 1984.

Yields 1 cup

WILD RICE WITH PEAS AND ONIONS

*¹/₃ cup wild rice, rinsed
   well and drained
2 tablespoons butter
¹/₂ cup chopped onion*

*¹/₂ cup fresh peas
2 teaspoons lemon juice
2 tablespoons minced
   fresh parsley
4 nasturtiums*

Cook the rice in 1 cup of water, covered, for forty to fifty minutes, or until tender. Melt butter and sauté onion three to four minutes. Add the peas and stir for several more minutes until tender but still crisp. Stir in the cooked rice, lemon juice and parsley. Simmer until heated through. Remove to serving dish and sprinkle with torn nasturtium petals.

Serves 2

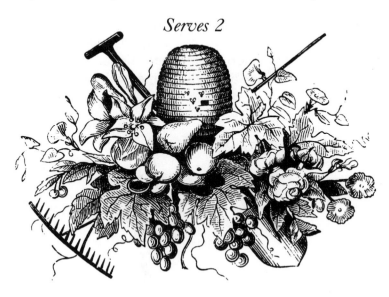

A GREAT GRAPE

*S*ir Walter Raleigh reportedly discovered the Scuppernong grape in 1584 on Roanoke Island, Virginia. The original vine, once called the "Walter Raleigh Vine," has become known as the "Mother Vine." Its gnarled trunk is now over two feet in diameter, and the vine still bears fruit.

"Scuppernong" is an Algonquin Indian word meaning place of the sweet bay tree. It was in the shade of these trees that the Scuppernong grape grew in profusion great enough to render it healthy and producing still. Thomas Jefferson was purported to be a devotee of the Scuppernong grape and the rich, amber wine it produced. He planted a number of vines at Monticello and proudly served the jelly as well as the wine.

Try Scuppernong Jelly on sourdough pancakes. Scuppernong wine is available in most liquor stores. It is a rich spicy wine close to a sherry that would be an unusual accompaniment to or ending for a wild game, wild greens meal.

WILD SCUPPERNONG JELLY

1 quart Scuppernong grapes   *Sugar*

Remove stems from Scuppernongs, wash and drain thoroughly. Mash grapes, a small amount at a time. Bring to a boil and boil one-half hour. Remove from heat, and strain juice through a jelly bag. Measure juice, then measure an equal amount of sugar. Return juice to a boil, and boil five minutes. Add sugar, stirring until dissolved. Cook rapidly until mixture sheets off a metal spoon.

Ladle jelly into hot sterilized glasses. Seal with a ⅛-inch layer of melted paraffin. When paraffin has cooled, top with another ⅛-inch layer.

Note: Try this with Concord grapes too.

WILD RASPBERRY JELLY

3 quarts wild raspberries, red or black
7 cups sugar

2 tablespoons lemon juice
1 cup liquid pectin

Crush raspberries and drip through jelly bag. Measure 4 cups juice. Combine raspberry juice, sugar, and lemon juice. Cook over high heat until mixture boils. Add pectin, stirring constantly. Remove from heat and skim. Pour into hot sterilized glasses. Cover with paraffin.

Makes 10 cups of jelly

WILD RASPBERRY JELLY ROLL

5 eggs, separated
1 cup sugar
3 tablespoons orange juice
1 cup sifted all-purpose
flour

1 teaspoon cornstarch
¹/₄ teaspoon salt
Confectioner's sugar
1 cup wild raspberry jelly

Beat egg whites until almost stiff. Add ¹/₂ cup sugar gradually, beating constantly until mixture is very stiff. Beat egg yolks until thick; add remaining ¹/₂ cup sugar gradually, beating constantly, until thick. Add orange juice. Fold egg yolk mixture into egg white mixture. Sift flour with salt and cornstarch. Add to egg mixture. Line a jelly roll pan with waxed paper. Grease the paper. Turn batter into 11" x 16" pan and spread evenly. Bake in 350° oven for 15 minutes. Turn out onto towel sprinkled with confectioner's sugar. Remove paper and trim crusts. Roll up and allow to cool. Unroll to spread with jelly, then reroll.

Serves 4

WILD STRAWBERRY FREEZER JAM

3 cups ripe wild
  strawberries
5 cups sugar

1 cup water
1 envelope powdered
  pectin

Mash berries, then add sugar slowly, stirring after each addition. Stir occasionally for 20 minutes to dissolve sugar. Boil the water and add the pectin. Return to boil and cook one minute, stirring constantly. Remove from heat. Add fruit. Stir another two minutes. Pour into sterilized jars. Cover. Let stand at room temperature 12 hours. Invert and allow to stand another 12 hours. Freeze.

This jam is as close to fresh berries as anything you can find. Served over cheesecake, on toast, fresh biscuits, or scrapple, or in a parfait with an orange brandy, it is absolutely superb. Well worth the time and effort.

Makes 5–6 cups jam

WILD STRAWBERRIES AND CREAM

2 cups wild strawberries   *4 hot biscuits*
2 cups cream

Gather and immediately clean the berries. Whip the cream until it is just beginning to thicken but not stiff. Crush the berries in a large bowl. Layer the berries and the cream in a shallow dish. Refrigerate overnight. Serve on hot biscuits.

Note: It's been said that this dish is so delectable that just eating it will make a poet of the lucky diner.

MAPLE SYRUP

aple sugar was used by the Indians to sweeten their food. Maple trees are tapped in early spring when the days start to warm and nights are still cold. Trees should be about 40 years old to be good sugar-producers, and most will go right on producing for a century or more. Maple sap is a delicate liquid that must be boiled down quickly before sun and air can develop bacteria that will mar its sweetness and flavor.

See venison section for *Venison with Maple Syrup.*

Note: Use pure maple syrup to sweeten fruit cup or grapefruit halves for a different taste treat. Add a little syrup to whipped cream to garnish waffles. Pour maple syrup over sliced bananas and top with whipped cream.

MAPLE SYRUP POPCORN

2 cups granulated sugar
2 cups pure maple syrup
1 teaspoon vinegar

2 tablespoons butter
1 cup chopped peanuts
4 quarts popped corn

Combine sugar, maple syrup, and vinegar, and cook over low heat, stirring until sugar dissolves. Cook to 275° on candy thermometer. Remove from heat. Add butter and stir until melted. Add peanuts and pour over popcorn. Blend well.

177

VERMONT MAPLE SYRUP EGGNOG

$^1/_3$ cup pure maple syrup
$^1/_8$ teaspoon salt
3 egg yolks, well beaten

2 cups milk
$^1/_2$ cup heavy cream
$^1/_8$ teaspoon ginger

Combine syrup, salt, egg yolks, and milk. Beat until blended. Pour into glasses. Combine cream and ginger, and top each serving with the mixture.

Serves 4

Down Home
Accompaniments

BRANCH ROAD SOURDOUGH

Starter
1 package active dry yeast
  (1 tablespoon)
2¹/₂ cups warm water
2 cups flour

1 tablespoon sugar
1 teaspoon salt

Dissolve yeast in ¹/₂ cup warm water. Stir in flour, sugar, and salt, and beat until smooth. Let stand, uncovered, at room temperature three to five days. Stir twice daily. Cover at night. The mixture will develop a yeasty smell. Refrigerate starter in crockery or glass jar until ready to use. To keep a new batch of starter each time you use some, add ¹/₂ cup water, ¹/₂ cup flour, and 1 teaspoon sugar to starter remaining after you have removed amount necessary for recipe. Again let stand until bubbly and fermented, at least one day. Store in refrigerator, and bring to room temperature before using.

Our first mountain home was located on Branch Road, in Promised Land. Many happy hours were spent, kneading, shaping, and watching sourdough rise on frosty weekends.

PROMISED LAND SOURDOUGH CHEESE AND ONION APPETIZERS

1 package active dry yeast
 (1 tablespoon)
1¹/₂ cups warm water
1 cup starter
2 teaspoons salt
2 teaspoons sugar
5 to 5¹/₂ cups flour

¹/₂ teaspoon baking soda
1 medium onion, finely
 chopped
¹/₂ cup grated sharp cheese
¹/₂ cup cream
¹/₄ cup cornmeal

Dissolve yeast in warm water. Add starter, salt, sugar, and half the flour. Beat well, cover, and let rise, about 90 minutes or until doubled. Combine soda with one cup flour and add to bread, mixing well. Turn out onto floured surface and knead five minutes, adding remaining flour as needed. Add onion, and knead three minutes. Add cheese and knead three more minutes. Form balls of dough the size of walnuts. Dip top of each ball into cream and then into cornmeal. Allow to rise until doubled in size. Bake at 350° until golden brown. Serve warm with cream cheese.

Note: This is an unusual and zippy appetizer, perfect as a prelude to a meal of wild game.

181

GRAMMY JENET'S RICH SCOTTISH TEA SCONES

1 tablespoon butter, softened
2 cups flour
2 teaspoons baking powder
¼ cup sugar
1 teaspoon salt
6 tablespoons very cold butter, cut into quarter-inch bits

1 egg
1 egg yolk
½ cup milk
¼ teaspoon vanilla
1 egg white

Coat a large baking sheet with the softened butter and set aside. Combine flour, baking powder, sugar, and salt in a large bowl. Add the butter bits, and rub the flour mix and butter together with your fingers until mixture is flaky. With a whisk, beat the egg and egg yolk together until they are frothy. Beat the milk and vanilla into the egg mix, and pour it over the flour mixture. With your hands or a large spoon, toss mixture together until the dough can be gathered into a ball. Dust lightly with flour on a lightly floured surface. Roll the dough out into a one-half-inch thick circle. With a cooky cutter or a glass, cut into two-inch rounds. Place the rounds about one inch apart on the baking sheet. With a fork, beat the egg white briskly, and brush some lightly over the tops of the scones. Bake in middle of preheated 400° oven for 15–20 minutes.

Makes 12

GRANDMA'S EDINBURGH SCONES

2 cups flour
3 tablespoons butter
1/2 teaspoon salt

1 egg
2 tablespoons milk
1 tablespoon sugar

Combine flour, butter, and salt with a pastry blender until mixture is the consistency of crumbs. Whisk the egg, milk, and sugar together, and stir into the flour mixture to make a soft dough. Roll out about 3/4-inch thick. Cut into triangles. Combine dough trimmings, reroll, and recut. Bake in center of 400° oven for ten minutes, or until edges turn golden. Be careful not to let bottoms burn.

GREAT SMOKIES CORNBREAD CAKES

1³/₄ *cups coarsely ground cornmeal (stone ground, preferably)*
1 cup water
1¹/₂ cups buttermilk
2 eggs, beaten

¹/₂ cup flour
1 tablespoon salt
1 teaspoon baking powder
¹/₄ teaspoon baking soda
¹/₄ cup melted butter

Combine cornmeal and water. Add buttermilk and beaten eggs. Sift together dry ingredients. Add to cornmeal mixture. This is a thin batter. Drop batter by spoonfuls onto hot lightly greased griddle to make small cakes. Turn once.

Serves 4

AUNT RUTH'S PERFECT PEAR PECAN BREAD

1/2 cup dark brown sugar
1/2 cup granulated sugar
1/2 cup vegetable oil
2 eggs
1/4 cup sour cream
1 teaspoon vanilla
2 cups flour
1 teaspoon baking soda
1/2 teaspoon salt
1/2 teaspoon cinnamon
1/4 teaspoon grated nutmeg

1 1/2 cups coarsely chopped unpeeled very ripe pears
2/3 cup coarsely chopped pecans
1/2 teaspoon finely grated lemon peel
Optional: Top batter with sesame seeds and push in gently

Preheat oven to 350°. Grease a 9 x 5-inch pan. Combine sugars and oil, and beat well. Add eggs, one at a time, beating well after each addition. Mix in sour cream and vanilla. Add dry ingredients and mix well. Stir in pears, pecans, and lemon peel. Spoon batter into the prepared pan. Bake until tester comes out clean, about one hour. Cool in pan ten minutes before turning out. Cook completely before slicing. Delicious topped with whipped cream cheese. Freezes well.

Note: This is perhaps the most delicious quick bread ever.

CRANBERRY BREAD

2 cups flour
1 cup sugar
1½ teaspoons baking
  powder
1 teaspoon salt
½ teaspoon baking soda
¼ cup butter or
  margarine, softened

¾ cup orange juice
1 tablespoon grated
  orange rind
1 egg, well beaten
2 cups fresh cranberries,
  chopped
½ cup chopped pecans or
  walnuts

Preheat oven to 350°.

Sift together all dry ingredients. Cut in butter until mix looks like cornmeal. Combine orange juice, grated rind, and egg, and add all at once to dry ingredients, mixing just enough to moisten. Fold in cranberries and nuts, mixing just until combined. Bake in greased 9 x 5 x 3-inch loaf pan one hour. Crust should be golden brown and cake tester come out clean. Store overnight in refrigerator for easier slicing.

Note: This is an excellent recipe for Thanksgiving dinner. To make delicious party sandwiches, spread thin slices with softened cream cheese and slice into fingers.

Variation: Make Blueberry Bread by substituting blueberries for the cranberries and adding ½ cup grated Cheddar in place of the nuts.

Serves 10–12

PERRY ROAD PANCAKES AND MAPLE SYRUP

1¹/₄ cups sifted flour
1 tablespoon baking
  powder
1 tablespoon sugar
¹/₂ teaspoon salt

1 egg, beaten
1 cup buttermilk
2 tablespoons vegetable oil
¹/₄ cup pure Vermont
  maple syrup

Sift together dry ingredients. Combine egg, buttermilk, and vegetable oil. Add to dry ingredients, and stir just until mixed. Bake on hot griddle. Makes about eight large pancakes. Top with Buttery Syrup.

BUTTERY SYRUP

1 cup pure Vermont
  maple syrup

4 tablespoons butter (one-
  half stick)

Melt butter in heavy saucepan. Add syrup and blend. Heat through, stirring constantly. Serve hot syrup mixture over pancakes—you'll find it doesn't cool the pancakes down and adds buttery goodness.

BENTON BUCKWHEAT CAKES

(From Starter)

1 cup lukewarm water
¹/₂ cup stirred buckwheat flour
¹/₂ cup sifted white flour
1 cup starter
2 tablespoons brown sugar

2 teaspoons pure maple syrup
¹/₂ teaspoon baking soda
¹/₂ teaspoon salt
1 tablespoon vegetable oil

Add water, buckwheat flour, and white flour to one cup of starter. Stir until smooth, let stand overnight. When ready to bake buckwheat cakes, add brown sugar, maple syrup, soda, and salt. Blend. Add oil.

When I was a little girl and waiting to move into our new house, my family and I lived in the Benton Hotel for several weeks. That grand hotel is gone now, but it was the most imposing structure in Benton, the quiet village in the endless mountains of Columbia County, PA., where I grew up. The country was strange enough to me, but stranger still was the yeasty, pungent odor about the dining room and kitchen each evening. The smell of buckwheat cakes rising permeated that old hotel, and I soon came to love them. They are different, strong-tasting and very satisfying.

O'DOUCHAIN'S MONTANA FRENCH TOAST

1 loaf French bread	6 eggs
2 ripe peaches	1/4 cup heavy cream
1/2 teaspoon cinnamon	6 tablespoons butter
1/2 cup sugar	1/2 cup maple syrup

Slice the bread into three-inch thick slices. Slit each slice through the middle to form a pocket. (Do not cut sides and bottom of bread.) Peel and chop the peaches. Combine the cinnamon and sugar. Toss the peaches in the spiced sugar, and spoon into the bread pockets. Press bread slices back together.

Beat eggs and add cream. Dredge stuffed bread slices in the egg mixture. Melt four tablespoons butter in large skillet. Fry the bread until toasted on both sides, turning carefully to retain the peach stuffing.

Melt the remaining butter in a small saucepan. Add the syrup and heat through, stirring to combine. Serve hot at the table to pour over French Toast.

Note: This is a breakfast befitting Montana's Big Sky country—and the O'Douchain Country Inn in Bigfork does everything Montana-style. We also liked the Inn's apple version of the above recipe. Substitute grated apples for the peaches, and the result is equally delicious.

Serves 4

AUNT MAG GINTHNER'S HOMEMADE NOODLES

4 eggs   *1 teaspoon salt*
2 cups flour

Water as needed (start with 1 tablespoon cold water, adding another if necessary to work dough).

Beat eggs until light. Add flour and salt. Dough will be very stiff and sticky. Add water. Mix until dough forms a ball. Turn out onto floured surface, and roll out until dough is very thin. Allow to rest one hour. Roll dough up like a jelly roll, and slice thin noodles.

You can also form dough for: *Pot Pie Noodles*

Roll thinly as above, and cut into one-inch squares. Use in any pot pie recipe.

Serving Suggestions

1. Buttered Noodles
Boil noodles until tender, 10–15 minutes depending on thickness of dough. Drain and rinse. Toss with melted butter.

2. Pennsylvania Dutch Buttered Noodles
Boil (10–15 minutes), drain, and rinse. Sauté bread cubes in butter until crisp. Toss noodles with melted butter and top with croutons.

3. Noodles Romanoff
Boil (10–15 minutes), drain, and rinse. Toss with 1 pint sour cream, 1 tablespoon Worcestershire sauce, and 1 clove crushed garlic. Top with 1 to 2 tablespoons cracker-meal, and bake at 350° until heated through. Can be made ahead and frozen.

KAREN'S BROCCOLI SUPREME

2 packages frozen chopped
  broccoli
2 packages frozen chopped
  spinach
2 cups sour cream
1 package dried onion
  soup mix

$^1/_2$ cup grated Cheddar
  cheese
$^1/_4$ cup crumbled blue
  cheese
$^1/_2$ cup grated Romano
  cheese

Thaw the broccoli and spinach in a large colander. Mix all the other ingredients together except the grated Romano. Pour into a four-quart baking dish. Top with Romano. Bake at 350° for 45 minutes, or until edges bubble and cheese turns golden.

Note: This is better if mixed a day in advance. My vegetable lovers rate this one a "ten," and any cook will love the easy, advance preparation.

Serves 6–8

JOYCE'S GOLDEN BAKED ONIONS

¹/₂ cup butter
6 medium onions, sliced
1 can cream of chicken
*   soup*
1 cup evaporated milk

¹/₄ teaspoon cayenne pepper
1 cup swiss cheese, grated
¹/₂ loaf french bread, sliced

Preheat oven to 350°. Grease a two-quart baking dish. Melt the butter in a large skillet over medium heat; add the onions and cook until tender and translucent, stirring frequently. Transfer onions to prepared dish, reserving the butter in the skillet. Combine soup, milk, salt and pepper in bowl, and pour over onions. Sprinkle with grated cheese. Dip bread slices in melted butter on one side. Arrange buttered side up over onion mixture to cover completely. Bake about thirty minutes, until bread is browned, and onions bubbly.

Serves 4

KAREN'S FAVORITE POTATO SALAD

½ cup salad oil
¼ cup vinegar
1 tablespoon salt
¼ teaspoon pepper
8 cups hot diced potatoes
¾ cup green olives,
    chopped

2 to 3 dill pickles,
    chopped
4 hard-cooked eggs, diced
2 cups diced celery
1 onion, chopped
1 cup salad dressing or
    mayonnaise

Mix together oil, vinegar, salt, and pepper. Pour over hot potatoes. Cool. Add remaining ingredients and chill.

Serves 6

MY FRIEND BETH'S LAYERED SALAD

1/2 medium head of
  lettuce, shredded
2 cups ripe cherry
  tomatoes, halved
1 cup ripe olives, if
  desired
2 cups fresh peas, cooked
1/2 cup chopped ham
1/2 cup green peppers,
  julienned

1/2 cup celery, diced
1 medium mild onion,
  thinly sliced and
  separated into rings
1 cup grated sharp
  Cheddar cheese
1 cup mayonnaise
1/2 pound bacon, fried
  crisp and crumbled for
  garnish

Assemble salad at least 2 hours before meal. You need a deep glass bowl to show this salad off properly.

Layer the ingredients, starting and ending with lettuce and leaving the grated cheese and bacon for last. Spread the top of the salad with mayonnaise (depending on the circumference of your bowl, you may need more than one cup). Make sure that the mayonnaise, about 3/4 inch thick, extends to the sides of the bowl to seal the salad.

Top with the grated cheese and refrigerate until serving time. Garnish with the bacon and serve immediately. Toss this salad at the table.

Note: I love being able to do as much ahead of time as possible, and here at last is a salad that will actually keep overnight. You can assemble this the day before serving and you will be amazed at how delicious and fresh it will be. Vary the vegetables to your taste.

Serves 6–8

CRANBERRY SALAD

$^1/_2$ cup crushed pineapple, drained

1 3 oz. package cherry gelatin dessert

1 16 oz. can whole berry cranberry sauce

1 rib celery, finely chopped

1 apple, finely chopped

$^1/_4$ cup chopped walnuts

Drain pineapple, saving juice. Measure juice and add enough boiling water to make one cup liquid. In medium-sized bowl, mix gelatin with boiling water according to directions. Stir well, add pineapple juice. Stir in cranberry sauce, and chill. When mixture is thick, add remaining ingredients, and pour into 9 × 13-inch pan. Chill. In one-half hour, stir to remix, and keep chilled.

Note: This is a delicious, beautiful salad or side dish. Very effective with ham or fowl.

Serves 6

STRAWBERRY MOLD

2 3 oz. packages
   strawberry gelatin
   dessert
1 8 oz. can crushed
   pineapple
1 package frozen
   strawberries

3 medium bananas
½ pint sour cream
½ cup finely crushed
   pecans

Dissolve gelatin in 1½ cups of boiling water. Add crushed pineapple and juice. Then add the strawberries with their juice and the mashed bananas. Pour half of mixture in a two-quart mold. Let set in refrigerator until firm. Do not refrigerate the other half. Spread sour cream and crushed pecans over molded half, then pour remaining mix over the sour cream, and refrigerate mold until set. Unmold to serve.

Serves 8

HOMEMADE BEEF BOUILLON

1 beef soup bone   *1 teaspoon salt*
1 pound beef, untrimmed   *$^{1}/_{2}$ teaspoon Accent*
1 large onion, whole   *1 teaspoon oregano*

Brown beef (with fat) in heavy skillet or kettle over medium heat at least one-half hour, stirring frequently. Each piece of beef should be browned, and the pan should be taking on a dark, golden color on the bottom. When meat is browned and some pieces are just at the point of burning, add 2 cups of water and lower heat. Stir until you have dislodged all the particles sticking to the bottom of the pan. Simmer another half hour with the bone and remaining ingredients. With a slotted spoon remove the meat and onion and allow the bone to remain in the pot. Boil on medium heat uncovered, until the liquid is reduced to 1 cup. This becomes the base for several recipes and can be considered condensed broth or bouillon.

COOPERSBURG CORN CHOWDER

1 medium onion, chopped
1 cup chopped celery
2 tablespoons butter or
   margarine
1 16 oz. can creamed
   corn
1 quart milk

2 cups grated sharp cheese
1 tablespoon seafood
   seasoning
1 teaspoon oregano
1 teaspoon basil
1 teaspoon paprika

Sauté the onion and celery in butter. Add remaining ingredients, and bring to boiling. Reduce heat immediately, and simmer 15 to 20 minutes to allow flavors to blend.

Note: This is a meal in itself, a very rich and satisfying soup.

Serves 6

JIMMY BRUD'S FAVORITE WHISKEY CAKE

4 eggs
1 cup milk
2 tablespoons whiskey
1/2 cup oil
1 cup walnuts, chopped

1 box yellow cake mix (plain, not pudding mix)
1 box vanilla instant pudding

Beat eggs, add liquid ingredients, and combine. Add remaining ingredients. Pour into greased and floured tube pan. Bake at 350° approximately one hour, or until tester comes out clean. Pour glaze over cake while the cake is still warm, not hot.

Serves 8–10

GLAZE

8 oz. butter (one stick)
3/4 cup sugar

1/2 cup whiskey

Melt butter in saucepan. Add sugar. Stir until dissolved. Remove from heat. Allow to cool five minutes. Add whiskey, and stir until blended. Poke holes in warm cake, still in pan, with skewer or toothpick. Pour glaze slowly over cake allowing it to soak in completely until you pour more. This takes some time. The whiskey flavor permeates the cake, making it moist and rich and wonderful. Invert when all glaze is used and cake is cool. Even cake haters love this one.

DELUXE VERY WICKED CHOCOLATE RUM PIE

6 oz. butter, softened (one
  and one-half sticks)
1 cup sugar
5 eggs
3 squares melted baking
  chocolate

¹/₃ cup rum (dark
  preferred)
1 baked and cooled 9" pie
  shell
1 cup whipped cream

Cream the butter and sugar in a blender. Do not use a mixer or food processor. Add the eggs and melted chocolate. Blend until dark and smooth. Add rum. Blend several more seconds. Pour into the pie shell, and refrigerate at least three hours. Garnish with whipped cream and chocolate curls, if desired.

Note: This is a very, very rich pie. Serve in small pieces. If made in the blender the filling has the consistency of a smooth chocolate bar. Food processor and mixer do not produce that consistency.

Serves 8

AUNT MARY'S SURPRISE BARS

1 cup sugar
8 oz. butter, softened
  (two sticks)
1/4 cup unsulfured
  molasses
1 egg yolk
1 teaspoon vanilla

2 cups flour
1 12 oz. package
  chocolate chips
1 cup seedless raisins
1 cup walnuts
1/3 cup creamy peanut
  butter

Mix sugar, butter, molasses, egg yolk, and vanilla until blended. Stir in flour and one cup of the chocolate chips. Press dough in ungreased 13 x 9 x 2-inch pan. Bake until golden 25 to 30 minutes. Mix remaining chocolate chips, raisins, nuts, and peanut butter in saucepan. Heat over medium-low heat, stirring constantly until chips are melted. Spread over crust in pan. Refrigerate at least two hours. Cut into bars.

Makes 4 1/2 dozen

JOE CAHN'S BREAD PUDDING

1 10 oz. loaf stale French
   bread, crumbled (or 6–
   8 cups any type bread)
4 cups milk
2 cups sugar
4 tablespoons butter,
   melted
3 eggs

2 tablespoons vanilla
1 cup raisins
1 cup cocoanut
1 cup chopped pecans
1 teaspoon cinnamon
1 teaspoon nutmeg

Combine all ingredients; mixture should be very moist but not soupy. Pour into buttered 9″ x 9″ baking dish. Place into non-preheated oven. Bake at 350° for approximately one hour and 15 minutes until top is golden brown. Serve warm with sauce.

Serves 16–20

WHISKEY SAUCE

¹/₂ cup butter (1 stick, ¹/₂ pound)
1¹/₂ cups powdered sugar

1 egg, yolk or whole (yolk preferred)
¹/₂ cup bourbon (to taste)

Cream butter and sugar over medium heat until all butter is absorbed. Remove from heat and blend in egg yolk. Pour in bourbon gradually to your own taste, stirring constantly. Sauce will thicken as it cools. Serve warm over warm bread pudding.

Note: For a variety of sauces, just substitute your favorite fruit juice or liqueur to complement your bread pudding.

MIL'S CHOCOLATE CHIP CUPCAKES

4 oz. butter or margarine
  (one stick)
6 tablespoons granulated
  sugar
6 tablespoons brown
  sugar
1 egg

$^1/_2$ teaspoon vanilla
1 cup plus 2 tablespoons
  flour
$^1/_2$ teaspoon baking soda
$^1/_2$ teaspoon salt

Beat butter, sugar, egg, and vanilla together until smooth. Sift the dry ingredients together, and add them to the liquid mixture. Fill cupcake tins one-third full and bake at 350° six minutes. Remove from oven and spoon one tablespoon of filling into each cupcake. Bake five minutes more. Center will be soft and chewy like a cooky.

Chocolate Chip Filling

1 egg
$^1/_2$ cup brown sugar

$^1/_2$ teaspoon vanilla
1 6 oz. package chocolate
  chips

Combine egg with brown sugar. Fold in remaining ingredients thoroughly.

Makes 2 dozen

SCOTCH SHORTBREAD

8 oz. butter (two sticks)
½ cup sugar
2½ cups flour
¼ teaspoon salt

¼ teaspoon almond
  flavoring
½ cup chopped almonds

Cream butter. Add sugar, then remaining ingredients, stirring in almonds last. Roll into a ball and chill 1 hour. Roll chilled dough 1″ thick on a floured board. Cut into squares or diamonds. Bake at 325° for 20 minutes. Prick top of each cooky all over with a fork after removing shortbread from oven.

Note: This is a rich, crisp cooky-like treat.

POCONO MOUNTAIN BLUEBERRY SYRUP/JAM

3 cups blueberries   *1 cup water*
5 cups sugar   *1 box powdered pectin*

Mash berries and add sugar, stirring constantly. Stir for at least 20 minutes to dissolve sugar. Boil water. Add pectin, and resume boil. Boil and stir for one minute. Remove from heat. Add fruit and stir for five minutes. Pour into jars. Cover and let stand at room temperature 24 to 48 hours. Invert jars after 12 hours. Store in freezer.

This syrup-jam is so delicious because the fruit is not cooked and it retains its fresh taste and texture. It is super on cheesecake, parfaits, ice cream, and pancakes. Will last up to six weeks after thawing, but never fear! It won't be around that long.

JANET VANCE'S MIRACLE BUTTERMILK PIE

1½ *cups sugar*
½ *cup Bisquick*
1 *cup buttermilk*

½ *cup melted butter*
3 *eggs, beaten*
1 *tablespoon vanilla*

Combine the dry ingredients in a bowl. Beat together buttermilk, butter, eggs and vanilla. Pour this mixture into the dry ingredients, stirring well to combine. Bake in an ungreased nine-inch pie pan at 350° for about thirty minutes or until tester comes out clean.

CHOCOLATE PECAN BUTTERMILK PIE

Add three tablespoons cocoa powder to the dry ingredients and stir in one-half cup chopped pecans after combining the buttermilk mixture. Bake as directed.

This is a very rich dessert sure to please the chocolate lover.